WALKS FOR ALL AGES
NORTHUMBERLAND

WALKS *FOR* ALL **AGES**

NORTHUMBERLAND

KATE SANDERSON

BRADWELL
BOOKS

Published by Bradwell Books
9 Orgreave Close Sheffield S13 9NP
Email: books@bradwellbooks.co.uk

British Library Cataloguing in Publication Data: a catalogue record for this book is available from the British Library.

1st Edition

ISBN: 9781909914223

Print: Gomer Press, Llandysul, Ceredigion SA44 4JL

Design by: Erik Siewko Creative, Derbyshire.
eriksiewko@gmail.com

Photograph Credits: © Kate Sanderson
and credited individually
Cover image: iStock.
Back Cover images: iStock

Maps: Contain Ordnance Survey data
© Crown copyright and database right 2014

Ordnance Survey licence number 100039353

The information in this book has been produced in good faith and is intended as a general guide. Bradwell Books and its authors have made all reasonable efforts to ensure that the details are correct at the time of publication. Bradwell Books and the author cannot accept any responsibility for any changes that have taken place subsequent to the book being published. It is the responsibility of individuals undertaking any of the walks listed in this publication to exercise due care and consideration for the health and wellbeing of each other in the party. Particular care should be taken if you are inexperienced. The walks in this book are not especially strenuous but individuals taking part should ensure they are fit and able to complete the walk before setting off.

WALKS FOR ALL AGES

INTRODUCTION

NORTHUMBERLAND IS A LARGE COUNTY WITH BIG SKIES AND FEW PEOPLE. THERE ARE MILES OF GLORIOUS BEACHES, DUNES, HARBOURS AND ISLANDS, AS WELL AS PRETTY VILLAGES AND MARKET TOWNS SET IN THE SPECTACULAR SCENERY OF THE CHEVIOT HILLS, DEEP VALLEYS, MOORLAND AND FOREST.

Kielder Water and Forest Park together with Northumberland National Park cover an amazing 580 square miles (1,500 sq. km), just a little less than London at 611 square miles. This area is designated an International Dark Sky Park, one of the largest in the world, making stargazing an awesome experience and benefiting the abundant wildlife.

The biggest man-made lake in northern Europe and the largest working forest in England are both to be found at Kielder. Hadrian's Wall is a World Heritage Site and there are many Roman remains and museums in this area. Castles, bastles and pele towers are littered around Northumberland as it was ravaged by the warring, upheaval and unrest of the Border Reivers for almost 300 years.

These walks have tried to give a flavour of these different landscapes and historic sites. Please check the opening times of the attractions mentioned in the directions as well as the times of the train at Heatherslaw and the ferry at Kielder. There is something special and interesting about all these walks and I hope you enjoy them.

ALNWICK

ALNWICK IS A TOWN STEEPED IN HISTORY AND THERE HAS BEEN A CASTLE HERE FOR OVER A THOUSAND YEARS. THE PRESENT CASTLE, HOME TO THE DUKE AND DUCHESS OF NORTHUMBERLAND, HAS BEEN IN THEIR FAMILY FOR OVER 700 YEARS. THIS IS AN INTERESTING CASTLE FOR FAMILIES TO VISIT AS THERE ARE MANY ACTIVITIES FOR CHILDREN.

Nearby is Alnwick Garden, which also caters for families, and children love the Cascade as the water jets shoot out unpredictably – all of a sudden there are loud screams as the children are showered with water. The Poison Garden is a favourite with older children and terrible tales are told by the guides to the delight of the visitors. For the serious gardener, the Ornamental Garden is a delight with its pleached trees and geometric beds.

Part of this walk is across the Pastures and it is said that, at certain times, the wind here sounds like tormented weeping and wailing. It may be the souls of the prisoners who were captured at the Battle of Dunbar in 1660 by Cromwell's army and imprisoned in the bailey of Alnwick Castle. Within the first week 3,000 prisoners died of starvation and disease and the rest were forced to march to Durham, but very few of the 6,000 survived the journey.

You can hardly miss the Tenantry Column as it is 83 feet (25m) in height with a lion on the top. In 1816 the second Duke of Northumberland kindly reduced the rents of his tenants, who thanked him by building this monument. However, the Duke then thought that if they could pay for a column they could pay their rents!

Across from the Tenantry Column in what was Alnwick's Railway Station is Barter Books, a second-hand bookshop. It has lots of railway features, and model railways run across the tops of the bookshelves. For a ride on a steam train visit the Aln Valley Railway at Lionheart Station. Check their website to see when trains are running at www.alnvalleyrailway.co.uk.

iStock

THE BASICS

Distance: 2½ miles / 4km
Gradient: A few small but steep hills in the town and across The Pastures
Severity: Easy
Approx time to walk: 2 hrs
Stiles: None
Maps: OS Explorer 332 (Alnwick & Amble)
Path description: Pavements in the town and grassy footpath across The Pastures
Start point: The car parks in Greenwell Road, Alnwick (GR NU 187133)
Parking: The main car parks are in Greenwell Road and there is some street parking in the town (NE66 1HB)
Dog friendly: Dogs on leads in the town and in The Pastures
Public toilets: Market Street, Alnwick
Nearest food: There are lots of cafes, pubs and sandwich shops in Alnwick. There are no refreshment stops across The Pastures so take some water with you

ALNWICK WALK

1. Start in the car park in Greenwell Road. Turn left as you leave the car park and walk along to the main road, Bondgate Without. Turn left past the Playhouse to the junction with the War Memorial. Cross here and take a walk round the Tenantry Column with the lion on the top. Go back to the junction and turn right along Denwick Lane. The entrance to the Alnwick Garden is on the left near the pedestrian traffic lights. Here there are toilets, a very nice gift shop, a fish and chip shop and the visitor centre. If you wish to enter the garden itself there is an admission charge. This walk continues along the road past the stone wall and when you cross the bridge over the River Aln you will see wooden gates on your left, a path and a sign to the Lion Bridge.

2. Go through the gates and follow the path across The Pastures. As you walk along there are good views of Alnwick Castle. The path can be a bit muddy in wet weather. After a while you come to a stile but if you look to your right, a little way along is a gate that you can use instead. Continue until you see the Lion Bridge and take the path up to the road. Turn left, crossing the bridge. You are now on The Peth and it is a bit of a climb until you get to the junction at Bailiffgate where there is a museum and the Parish Church. This walk continues with the entrance to Alnwick Castle on your left and follows Narrowgate. As you walk along you will see the pant (water fountain) on your right at the bottom of Pottergate. Continue along Narrowgate until you come to a narrow lane called Paikes Street. It is pretty here and it takes you to the Market Square with the 18th-century Town Hall and clock tower on your right. To your left is the impressive Northumberland Hall gifted to the town by the Duke of Northumberland in 1919.

3. Walk along until you come to Market Street, turn left and here you will find toilets and the Tourist Information Centre in the arcade under the Northumberland Hall.

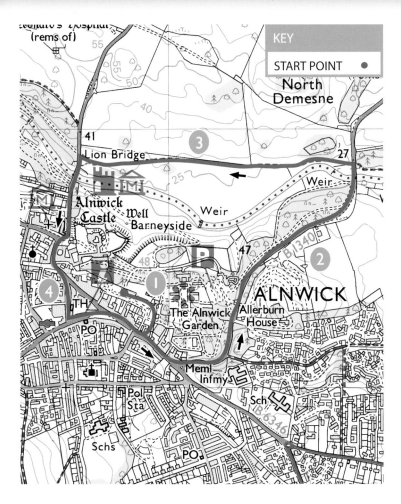

4. You will see the cobbled parking area on your right. Continue to the junction, and turn right into Bondgate Within. You pass the White Swan Hotel on your left. Go through the Hotspur Tower archway into Bondgate Without and take the first left into Greenwell Road and return to the car park.

AMBLE & WARKWORTH

Amble, which lies a mile-and-a-half south-east of Warkworth, owes its past prosperity to the 18th and 19th-century coal trade. Vast quantities of coal were exported with large shipments going to London.

Exports of coal in 1854 were 78,000 tons and by 1880 this had increased to 187,000 tons. By 1884 it took 691 vessels to transport the 226,000 tons of coal. Exports in 1880 included 700,000 bricks, 1,787 barrels of herring and 620 tons of stone. The Romans also settled here and in 1856 a ploughman turned up broken pieces of an altar bearing the inscription, 'To the Campestral mothers by the first Cohort', in a field at Gloster Hill.

The ancient village of Warkworth, Amble's picturesque neighbour, is dominated by the remains of a motte and bailey castle, the birthplace of Harry Hotspur and the setting for some scenes of Shakespeare's Henry IV. The many daffodils planted around the castle mound are a magnificent sight in the spring. The village, situated at the base of a steep incline, is set in a horseshoe bend formed by the River Coquet with the main street, Castle Street, leading up to the castle.

Warkworth is an extremely popular place on the tourist route with several pubs and tearooms. Car parking can be found on the riverside by driving through the village square and passing between the church and the houses on the left. On sunny days this is one of the best villages to stroll around after lunch in one of the local eateries.

THE BASICS

Distance: 3½ miles / 5.6km

Gradient: Short inclines

Severity: Easy

Approx time to walk: 2 hrs

Stiles: None

Maps: OS Explorer 332 (Alnwick & Amble)

Path description: Pavements, roads and tracks

Start point: Amble Car Park in Town Square near the Tourist Information Centre (GR NU 266045)

Parking: Several car parks in Amble and on the Braid (NE65 0DQ)

Dog friendly: Dogs on leads

Public toilets: At Amble Tourist Information Centre and in Warkworth village

Nearest food: Cafes and pubs in both Warkworth and Amble. Choice of places to buy picnic food in Amble

AMBLE & WARKWORTH WALK

1. Start at the car park in Amble in the town square, near the Tourist Information Centre. With your back to the TIC turn left up Queen Street.

2. Bear right at the top, with the Co-op on the right-hand corner and the Wellwood Pub opposite. Keep on the right-hand side walking around the corner. You are now on The Wynd.

3. At the first opportunity cross the road, then turn left and follow the road up Gloster Hill. There is a small housing development on your left. Keep on the road and beware of oncoming traffic. Although traffic is very light, it is an ever present danger so where possible walk on the right-hand side facing oncoming cars.

4. At the top of the hill on your left, just behind a low wall are two stone piers, all that remains of the old manor house, burnt down on Sunday 7 January 1759. On careful examination you might just be able to discern carvings of two lion's claws. Looking to the right there is a view towards the Coquet and Warkworth Castle. Walk on passing Gloster Hill Farm on your left and cottages on the right and stop at the road junction.

5. Turn right here heading towards Warkworth village. A few yards down the road there is a World War II pillbox, constructed in local sandstone to blend into the countryside. From here the road dips into a series of bends. Proceed straight on to the western edge of the village, passing a school on your right.

6. At the T-junction turn left up Morwick Road; the road sign reads Acklington. Approximately 100 yards up Morwick Road, opposite number 72, there is a public footpath accessed through a large gap in a hedge.

7. Go to the end of this short section, turn left and proceed to the end, passing back gardens on the left and an open field on the right. At the gate turn right, passing a cottage with a millstone leaning against the wall, and walk on to the end of the road until you reach two cottages in the shadow of a large sycamore tree.

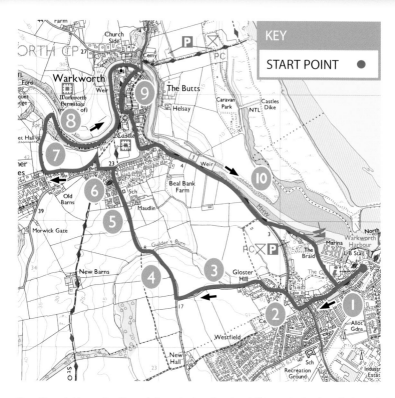

8.   Bear right, passing through the gate, heading downhill towards the river. At the end turn right (the way sign reads Mill Walk), and proceed along the path parallel to the river. This is a longish path leading to Warkworth village church. On the way keep an eye out for herons on the river. Further along you come to a boat-hire landing stage. Here, at the fork in the path, carry straight on. The river is on your left. Carry on with the church on your right; the sign reads Monks Walk. Head for the 14th-century fortified bridge.

9.   Turn right here and start walking through the village. Follow the road up through the village, with the castle on your right, and take the next left signposted Amble.

10. Walk down the road towards Amble, with the river on your left. Just before reaching Amble there is an opening in the fence and a signpost saying Coastal Path; follow the path over the grass heading for the Coquet Yacht Club. Continue through the boat yard and around the edge of the marina basin. Keep on this path, crossing the access road into the marina, and follow the sign for the town centre. You will arrive at the middle of Queen Street. Turn left here and head back down to the car park.

BERWICK-UPON-TWEED

BERWICK-UPON-TWEED IS DESCRIBED BY ART HISTORIAN SIR NIKOLAUS PEVSNER IN *THE BUILDINGS OF ENGLAND* AS 'ONE OF THE MOST EXCITING TOWNS IN ENGLAND, A REAL TOWN, WITH THE STRONGEST SENSE OF ENCLOSURE, A TOWN OF RED ROOFS ON GREY HOUSES WITH HARDLY ANY IRRITATING BUILDINGS ANYWHERE'.

Berwick is the only walled town in Britain where the walls are still complete. The ramparts and bastions were built between 1558 and 1570, during the reign of Queen Elizabeth I, and these amazing earth ramparts are 50 feet (15m) thick and faced with stone. During this walk you will experience the views from the top of the ramparts, and see the flankers, where the hidden guns waited to blast the approaching enemy, and the Magazine, where the gunpowder was stored.

This English Heritage site has free access and very good information panels that describe how the ramparts and bastions were built, the type of artillery used and other interesting facts, so they will not be explained in detail here. At one point there is the opportunity to visit Berwick Barracks built in the 18th century by Hawksmoor, which is also an English Heritage attraction (there is an admission charge).

Near the beginning of the route you will see the entrance to the Bankhill Georgian Ice House where ice was stored in the winter months and later used to pack the salmon to keep it fresh on its journey to the grand houses in London. Ice was gathered from the river and local lakes but by the 20th century much of the ice was brought by ship from Norway and the last ice-ship docked in Berwick in 1939. One of the main exports from Berwick was grain – barley in particular – and you will see the 18th-century Dewar's Lane Granary towards the end of your walk.

It is now an art gallery, bistro and youth hostel. Directions begin and end at the 18th-century Town Hall.

THE BASICS

Distance: 2½ miles / 4km

Gradient: Several steep but short inclines and some steps

Severity: Easy

Approx time to walk: 2 hrs

Stiles: None

Maps: OS Explorer 346 (Berwick-upon-Tweed)

Path description: Mainly tarmacked footpaths, a few grassy sections and pavements in the town

Start Point: The Town Hall, Marygate, Berwick-upon-Tweed (GR NT 998529)

Parking: Variety of town centre car parks (TD15 1BN)

Dog friendly: Dogs on leads in the town and on ramparts as there are steep drops

Public toilets: In the car park in Castlegate and in the Woolmarket

Nearest food: There is a good variety of cafés and pubs in the town and shops to buy sandwiches

BERWICK-UPON-TWEED WALK

1. Start by the steps outside the Town Hall in Marygate, cross the road and turn left down West Street. At the bottom turn right into Love Lane. Take the right-hand path signed as 'The Tweed Footpath to Letham Plantation'.

2. On your right is Berwick Ice House. Continue along and under the Royal Tweed Bridge. The Leaping Salmon Pub is on your right.

3. On your left is a statue of Annie, Lady Jerningham and her dogs. There are good views of the three bridges here: the Old Bridge, the Royal Tweed Bridge and on your right the Royal Border Railway Viaduct. The road bears right and you will see the Loovre Café, built as a loo in 1899. It still has a Minton tiled floor and sells local ice cream and hot and cold drinks.

4. Go through the iron gates on your left onto the ramparts, turn left up some steps to Megs Mount for good views of the Tweed estuary, Tweedmouth, Spittal and, in the distance, the castles of Lindisfarne and Bamburgh. Return to the footpath and go left to Scots Gate. Here you can see Marygate and the Town Hall and on the other side Castlegate. In the 16th century, the walled town was reduced and these new ramparts were built. The Main Guard once stood here and the soldiers secured the town every night. In 1816 it was moved to Palace Street.

5. Continue along and take the right-hand low footpath and you will come to the Cumberland Bastion, one of the five gun platforms. Take the high path and look down to see where the guns where sited.

6. At Brass Bastion turn left up the grassy path between the hillocks for good views. Return to the footpath and continue left – look down and see the flankers, two sunken stone chambers that held hidden guns.

7. Turn right down towards the Gymnasium Galley. Behind it is Berwick Barracks, an English Heritage site (admission charge).

8. The walk continues with the Gymnasium Gallery on your right. At Windmill Bastion (there used to be a windmill where the Lion House now stands) turn left along the wide grassy path and you will see the gun placements and information about the volunteer gunners. Continue walking round the Bastion and you will see Berwick lighthouse. You end up back on the footpath. Go left and take the low path.

9. On your right is the Magazine, the gunpowder store. Between here and the allotments is a house with lions on the gateposts. The famous artist L.S. Lowry, a frequent visitor to Berwick, considered buying this house but didn't do so in the end.

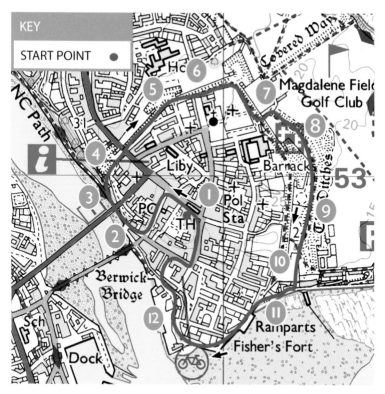

KEY

START POINT ●

10. Continue along with the allotments on your right and go through the iron gates. These riverside walls are part of Berwick's medieval defences and you will see a cannon at Fisher's Fort that was brought back from the Crimean War (1854–6). There is a double-headed eagle embossed on top of the barrel, the emblem of the Russian Tsar.

11. Continue straight on to Coxton's Tower gun platform. A little further along is a right-hand turn and near the corner is the Main Guard. Continue along and down some stairs into Sandgate.

12. Continue along until you come to some steps on your right-hand side. Go down the steps to Dewar's Lane Granary with a café and exhibition space. Walk through the courtyard and turn right into the lane and then right into Bridge Street. At the junction turn left up Hide Hill and at the top you will see the Town Hall.

CRASTER & DUNSTANBURGH CASTLE

CRASTER IS A FISHING VILLAGE WITH STONE COTTAGES, ROOFED IN RED TILE OR SLATE. THE ORIGINAL PLAN FOR BUILDING THE HARBOUR WAS FOR A SELF-FINANCING PROJECT FROM THE SALE OF AN ESTIMATED 79,000 TONS OF ROCK EXCAVATED TO CREATE THE HARBOUR AND A FURTHER 11,000 TONS FROM OUTSIDE THE IMMEDIATE HARBOUR AREA.

This idea came to a halt due to a lack of confidence in the financial viability of the project. The Craster family, not to be put off, managed to raise money from various family members as a memorial to a brother, John, with additional funds coming from the English Board of Trade and the Scottish Fishery Board. The concrete arch we see today once supported three silos for storing whinstone chippings carried in skips by an aerial ropeway from the quarry. Ships were loaded with chippings by chutes from the silos.

Dunstanburgh Castle is seated on a dark-pillared crop of the Whin Sill, which here is about forty feet (12m) thick, overlying beds of sandstone and shale, part of the Mountain Limestone formation. Many of the fissures in the basalt are filled with metamorphosed shale and sandstones, and in these patches various coloured quartz crystals can be found, known as 'Dunstanbrugh diamonds'.

The castle was built by Thomas, Earl of Lancaster, from 1314, who received a 'licence to crenellate' (i.e. permission to fortify his property) from the king in 1315. The position of the castle gained importance after the Scots recaptured Berwick in 1318. In 1322, Earl Thomas was executed for having 'secret dealings with the Scots'. During these troubled times the castle was taken and retaken five times, and as artillery was used in these successive sieges, the castle was left in a ruinous state. On the west side of the castle is the striking Lilburn Tower, most likely built by John Lilburn, constable of Dunstanburgh, around 1325. The tower stands with tall basaltic columns in front, like stone sentinels keeping a watchful eye on the grazing sheep below.

THE BASICS

Distance: 4 miles / 6.4km

Gradient: Short incline and stony parches around castle, otherwise flat

Severity: Easy

Approx time to walk: 2 hrs

Stiles: None

Maps: OS Explorer 332 (Alnwick & Amble)

Path description: Field track (well worn) and some roads

Start point: Craster car park (GR NU 256197)

Parking: Craster car park (NE66 3TW)

Dog friendly: Dogs must be on leads due to cattle, sheep and golfers

Public toilets: Craster car park

Nearest food: Dunstanburgh Golf Club and Craster Village with the Jolly Fisherman Pub and Robson & Sons Smokehouse shop and restaurant

1. This walk starts at the entrance to the car park in Craster. Turn right and head towards the harbour, keeping left and walking along the short stretch of road past some cottages on the left and through the wooden gate.

2. Head for Dunstanburgh Castle. The path is well worn and passes through another gate. Because sheep and cattle graze here, dogs must be kept on a lead and under control. After passing through the last gate, the path, which is a little rough here, winds to the left, towards the castle.

3. On reaching the castle entrance bear left, taking the narrow path. Take care here as the path is stony and uneven in places. As you descend there is a good view of Embleton Bay and Low Newton with the golf course on your left. At this point you can see the coast path ahead, dipping down and twisting over the brow of the hill, and on your left is a putting green. For this walk, because of erosion and general wear to the path ahead, follow the diversion at this point.

4. Walk round the edge of the putting green and head for the gravel path on the opposite side. A few yards along, this path divides in two. Take the left-hand grassy path which runs parallel to the fence with the golf course on your right. This is a longish stretch, all on grass, and at the end you have a choice. Either turn left through the gate up to Dunstan Steads or carry on to Dunstanburgh Golf Club. The clubhouse serves good food, there are customer toilets, and dogs are welcome at the outside tables. It is a five-to-ten-minute walk and you will return to this point later.

5. The path to the clubhouse passes through a short stand of trees and ends at a putting green. Keep to the left, and immediately on your left is the clubhouse and car park.

6. When ready, return to the gate for Dunstan Steads. Pass through the gate, walk a few yards up the road until you come to the steadings, which are now holiday cottages, and turn sharp left at sign marked Public Bridleway – Dunstan Square 1 Mile. As you walk along, the steadings are on your right and farm barns on the left. Ahead there is a field gate which takes you onto a concrete farm road, a continuation of the public bridleway.

7. You eventually come to the first of two cattle grids. On the left there are the remains of a lime kiln. Further along, there are the remains of a World War II pillbox on the right and on the left, a view of the castle in the distance and the second cattle grid.

8. You will now be approaching a small farmyard. Just after entering the yard, turn sharp

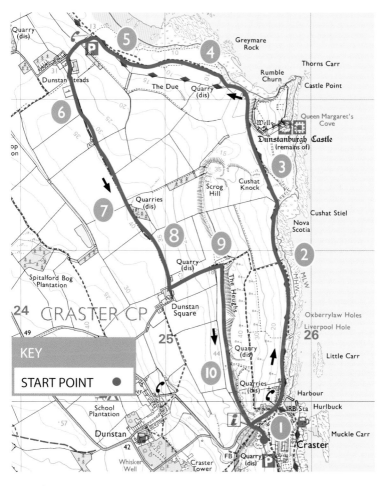

left at the end of the fence, where there is a signpost indicating Public Footpath, Dunstanburgh Castle. Pass through the gate.

9. Walk down the field and as you approach the bottom there is a gate on the right marked with a yellow arrow indicating a public footpath. Go through the gate and proceed along the path, which at this point looks rough and stony but soon gives way into an easier walk through the field.

10. Continue walking and the path eventually narrows as it passes through a wooded area finishing at a wooden gate opening onto the road; the car park is opposite. However, a visit to the village is recommended with its Jolly Fisherman Pub and Craster Smokehouse.

CORBRIDGE

This is a short walk around a Northumberland village with an optional visit to the Corbridge Roman Site.

This village is on my list of top three places in Northumberland along with Bamburgh and Holy Island. It is a stunning stone-built village which manages to impress and still be friendly and welcoming with lots of independent traders, good food and quality shops.

The streets are much as they were in medieval times and the attractive 17th-century bridge gives good views up and down the river. As a busy market town, Corbridge has

some very old inns such as the 17th-century Angel Inn, the Golden Lion and the Black Bull which date from the 1700s. In the nineteenth century, the main trades here were shoemaking and market gardening and many people were also employed in the lime industry and the iron works.

During the walk you tread the same street as the Romans, Watling Street, which appears to have once been called Dere Street, the famous Roman Road that ran from York to the Firth of Forth. Stanegate, a medieval name but a roman route, links Corbridge with Carlisle and runs past the fort of Vindolanda near Hadrian's Wall. The hub for these trade and military supply routes was Corstopitum, a large Roman supply camp. This was an essential store base

and market for the armies who guarded Hadrian's Wall and the civilians who supplied services to the military. If you are interested in the history of the Romans and Hadrian's Wall do visit Corbridge Roman Site by choosing the option at Watling Street; or if you wish to drive here you can go back to the car park and follow the signs.

When the Roman Camp was abandoned some of the stones were recycled in the 1300s to build the Vicar's Pele Tower in the village, and the vicar lived in this fortified house until the 1700s.

The Corbridge Roman Site is at Corchester Lane, NE45 5NT, and is maintained by English Heritage. There is an admission charge and you should check opening times before you set out.

THE BASICS

Distance: 1½ miles / 2.4km or 3 miles / 4.8km

Gradient: A little hilly in places

Severity: Easy

Approx time to walk: 1½ to 3 hrs if you go to the museum

Stiles: None

Maps: OS Explorer OL 43 (Hadrian's Wall)

Path description: Pavements and roads

Start point: Corbridge Village Car Park (GR NY 988640)

Parking: Corbridge Village Car Park, Station Road (NE45 5AX)

Dog friendly: Dogs on leads

Public toilets: Princes Street, Corbridge

Nearest food: Plenty of lovely teashops and good pubs

CORBRIDGE WALK

1. Turn left when you leave the car park and walk over the bridge. There are good views up and down the river from here. At the Angel Inn turn left along Middle Street with its quality fashion and accessories shops, the Black Bull Pub and Massey's Traditional Tearoom. It's hard to pass Grants with their amazing meringues!

2. When you arrive in the Market Place you'll see the old pant (water fountain) and the monument to Hugh Percy, Duke of Northumberland. On your right is St Andrew's Church. Turn right up the lane at the side of the church and along here you will see the old Market Cross. Turn right into Hill Street. When you arrive at the Tourist Information Centre cross the road and have a look at the Golden Lion, built with the stones from Dilston Hall.

3. Turn left into Princes Street and you will see the old Town Hall. Turn first left into St Helen's Street with its lovely stone cottages. Walk along until you come to Watling Street. If you do not wish to walk to the Roman Site, turn left and go to number 6.

4. To walk to Corbridge Roman Site, about three-quarters of a mile (1km), turn right and continue along. Watling Street becomes Stagshaw Road. Continue until you come to Corchester Lane on your left. Walk along Corchester Lane for about half a mile and the Roman Site is on your left. On leaving turn right and follow the road back to Watling Street and turn right.

5. Walk down here and you will arrive back in the Market Place.

6. Cross the Market Place and walk along Front Street, which is near the Forum Bookshop. At the end of the street turn right and walk back over the Corbridge Bridge to the car park.

7. To drive to Corbridge Roman Site follow the signs from the car park.

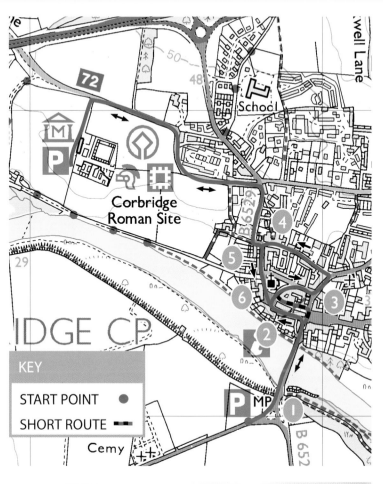

KEY

START POINT •

SHORT ROUTE ▪▪▪

THE GRACE DARLING WALK

One winter day, in a dull classroom in Glasgow, many years ago, we read Grace Darling, Heroine of the Farne Islands, and I was enthralled that such a brave young girl could face the stormy seas and rescue the poor people stranded on the Farnes in 1838.

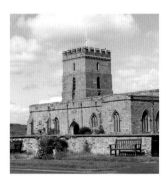

In Glasgow we knew all about bad weather and rough seas, and what she achieved in a small open fishing boat called a coble seemed an impossible task. On this walk you can follow her story, though not in chronological order.

Grace was born three doors down from the Grace Darling Museum and you can just make out the plaque above the door. The museum is free, so visit it first and see the model of the Longstone Lighthouse and the coble that she rowed to the rescue of the survivors of the shipwrecked *SS Forfarshire*. Grace was one of the first people to be made famous by the media and there are lots of souvenirs in the cabinets upstairs.

In Bamburgh village there is the cottage where Grace died and her memorial is in the churchyard opposite the Museum. The original is inside the church, where there is also a stained glass window in her honour. At Seahouses you can book a boat trip round the Farne Islands on Serenity (www.farneislandstours.co.uk) and see the red and white Longstone Lighthouse. Golden Gate Boats run special guided tours of the lighthouse and you can see Grace's room where she spotted, through her window, the nine survivors clinging to the rocks on a stormy night. However, there are many steep, worn and uneven steps and children need to be able to walk all the way up and down as they cannot be carried on the staircases; and you will need to wear sensible footwear. All the boat trips from Seahouses harbour depend on the tides, so make enquires before you plan your day.

The *Grace Darling*, a Mersey class lifeboat, can be seen in the RNLI lifeboat station near the harbour when it is open to the public and she is not out at sea. In the 18th century, Dr Sharpe commissioned a lifeboat from Lionel Lukin, designer of the world's first 'unimmergible', i.e. supposedly unsinkable, boat. Lukin adapted a coble and from 1789 this new lifeboat was in use at Bamburgh. There is more information about Dr Sharp at www. lordcrewescharity.org.uk.

NOTES: The Victoria Hotel in Bamburgh and the Bamburgh Castle Inn in Seahouses welcome dogs. There is no refreshment in between Bamburgh and Seahouses so take some water with you.

THE BASICS

Distance: 2½ miles / 4km or 6 miles / 9.6km

Gradient: Mostly flat but short uphill and downhill stretches over the dunes

Severity: Easy

Approx time to walk: 2 hrs or 4 hrs

Stiles: None

Maps: OS Explorer 340 (Holy Island & Bamburgh)

Path description: Pavements in the villages, tarmacked footpaths, a long stretch of sandy beach

Start point: The Grace Darling Museum, Bamburgh (GR NU 176348)

Parking: Bamburgh village (NE69 7AE)

Dog friendly: Dogs on leads in the villages and near roads

Public toilets: On the church side of The Grove in Bamburgh, in the car park between Bamburgh and Seahouses, and opposite the Tourist Information Office in Seahouses

Nearest food: Cafés, pubs and sandwich shops in both Bamburgh and Seahouses

THE GRACE DARLING WALK

1. Start at the RNLI Grace Darling Museum in Bamburgh, opposite the church, and have a look around. The cottage where Grace Darling was born is the third door on the left down from the museum. When you leave the museum turn right and then first right and then next left. The cottage where Grace died is next door to The Pantry, near the telephone box. There are public toilets on the far side of The Grove. Continue walking down towards Bamburgh Castle and follow the main road to the right. Behind the car park are the remains of an old dovecote.

2. Continue along the pavement and you will come to some green timbered cottages. These are Armstrong Cottages which were originally built as accommodation for the workers who were restoring the castle in the 19th century. On the other side of the road is a large car park. Cross the road and walk through the car park to the toilet block.

3. Outside the 'Ladies' is a wooden gate. Go through the gate and turn right along a well-used sandy path that heads towards the dunes. Follow the twists and turns of this path, looking out for wild flowers and grasses. When you come to a clearing, look left for a good view of Bamburgh Castle. This path bears right and then through a wooden gate and up over the dunes. Suddenly, you get a magnificent view of the sea and the Inner Farne with its white lighthouse and St Cuthbert's Chapel. In the distance is the red and white Longstone Lighthouse where the Darling family lived.

4. It is now time to choose whether to go on the long walk by turning right along the beach to Seahouses or to take the short walk and turn left back to Bamburgh. If you are going to return to Bamburgh go to number 8.

5. Turn right towards Seahouses and walk along the beach and over Greenhill Rocks. The dunes along here can be up to 100 feet (30m) high. Continue along the beach and you will see some cottages set back; this is Monks' House. The monks of Lindisfarne took their supplies from here to their cell on the Farne Islands. Continue along the beach and Seahouses will come into view. There is a well-trodden path across the dunes as you approach Seahouses and if you follow this up and over you will come out on the main road. Turn left towards Seahouses and the harbour. There are public toilets opposite the Tourist Information Office.

6. On the harbour at Seahouses is the RNLI Lifeboat Station and lots of kiosks offering boat trips to the Farne Islands and to Longstone Lighthouse. Seahouses is famous for its fish and chips and there are plenty of cafes and pubs. Dogs are welcome at the Bamburgh Castle Inn.

7. When you are ready to leave Seahouses return the way you came, back along the beach to where you turned right on the long walk.

8. Walk along the beach and you will see Bamburgh Castle on your left-hand side and just make out Lindisfarne Castle on Holy Island. It was along this beach that the world's first coastguard system was set up in 1781 by Dr John Sharp (1722–92). The coastguard's duties included riding along the beach during great storms to assist shipwrecked survivors, offering them shelter and food in Bamburgh Castle for seven days, storing cargo from shipwrecks and burying the dead. The massive iron chains used to rescue ships can be seen at Bamburgh Castle.

9. Just past the windmill (with no sails) at the far end of Bamburgh Castle take the well-trodden path up the sand dunes and follow it to the village. At the cricket field turn right and follow the path round to the main road. Turn right at the gate and keep on this side of the road and you will reach St Aiden's Church with Grace Darling's memorial in the churchyard. The original memorial is inside the church. Grace is buried, along with her family, in a small plot.

HARESHAW LINN & BELLINGHAM

THIS IS MORE A 'THERE AND BACK' WALK THAN A CIRCULAR ROUTE BUT IT IS ONE OF THE ICONIC WALKS IN NORTHUMBERLAND, LONG ENJOYED BY FAMILIES, AND IT IS WORTH THE STEEP CLIMB TO SEE THIS SPECTACULAR WATERFALL IN NORTHUMBERLAND NATIONAL PARK. YOU CERTAINLY GET A DIFFERENT VIEW ON THE WAY UP THAN ON THE WAY BACK DOWN, WHICH NEVER SEEMS TO TAKE SO LONG.

You will tread some paths made by the Victorians from stones collected from the bankside; and when they held picnics here, violin and accordion music would drift and echo along the gorge. You too can have a picnic as there are tables and benches near the beginning of the walk and seating areas along the way.

Between 1839 and 1849 there was an ironworks employing 500 workers by the Hareshaw Burn. The firm of Campion and Baston smelted iron here but the transport costs were prohibitive and the Union Bank took over the works when the company could not pay off its debts. They built two more furnaces but the business was not economic, so the works closed in 1849. The small car park at the beginning of the walk is where the old brickworks and stables once stood. However, when it was in operation these works produced good-quality iron which was used in the building of Newcastle upon Tyne's High Level Bridge.

This is an area of Special Scientific Interest as it is a haven for wildlife such as red squirrels, bats, badgers and the great spotted woodpecker. Most importantly, this ancient woodland has an outstanding collection of over 300 mosses, liverworts and lichens.

The Heritage Centre will give you an insight into the history of the area, and while walking round Bellingham, look at the roof of the 12th-century St Cuthbert's Church.

It is made of stone so that the Border Reivers could not set it on fire, as Bellingham was terrorised by the marauding Scots. In Lock Up Lane there is an interesting second-hand bookshop and this narrow lane was once used as a night lock-up for riotous and unruly people.

THE BASICS

Distance: 3¾ miles / 6km

Gradient: Hilly, steep in places

Severity: Easy, but more challenging due to hills and stone steps

Approx time to walk: 3 hrs

Stiles: None

Map: OS Explorer OL 42 (Kielder Water & Forest)

Path description: Pavements, forest tracks, stony paths and very steep stone steps

Start point: Heritage Centre car park, Bellingham (GR NY 841833)

Parking: Heritage Centre car park, Bellingham (NE48 2DG)

Dog friendly: Dogs on leads near roads and where sheep grazing

Public toilets: Bellingham

Nearest food: Carriages Tea Room at the Heritage Centre and pubs and cafés in Bellingham

HARESHAW LINN WALK

1. Start in the Heritage Centre in Bellingham and perhaps have a look around now or at the end of your walk. The Carriages Tea Room is an interesting place and you can enjoy meals or snacks sitting in these old railway carriages. All the food is prepared and cooked on the train. When you leave the car park turn left and walk down the hill to the bridge.

2. Turn right at this side of the bridge. You will see a sign for Hareshaw Linn. On your right-hand side is Joe's Seat, a memorial to P.C. Joe Carroll, who was killed on duty on 13 April 2006. The police station used to be across the road from here but it is now closed.

3. Walk along with the burn on your left. You will see the small car park where the brickworks and stables used to be. Continue straight on.

4. On the right, the building used to be the ironworks manager's offices. Keep walking straight ahead up the road.

5. On the left-hand side you will see an information board about the old ironworks. Continue uphill on the wide path and after a while the area will open out and there are picnic tables and seats. Continue straight on and there are a few stone steps. There is a sign reading 'Waterfall 1 mile'.

6. Continue on the path through the woodland. The path gets steeper and there are more steps and you come to a small bridge. Continue and you will come to a larger bridge which is called the First Bridge and you begin to see the water rushing along.

7. The path is more uneven now and the bridges come in quick succession: the second, then the third (we are counting from the one that said first bridge), the fourth, the fifth and the sixth.

8. There are steep steps here and a climb to the top and the seventh bridge. Watch out here as it can be muddy and very slippery.

9. The eighth wooden bridge has bends and a good view of the waterfall. Don't stop here as it is more dramatic a bit further along. Go down some more steps and continue along the path which opens out into a gorge – and there is the waterfall. You can walk down to the bottom of the waterfall but be very careful, especially if you have children with you.

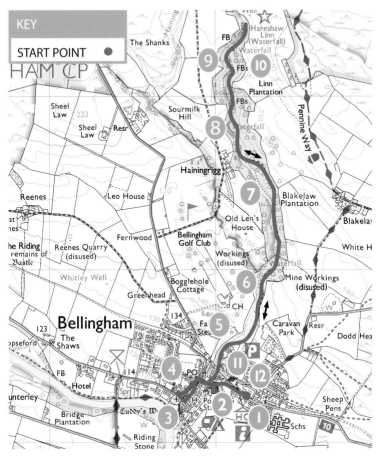

10. Go back the way you came until you reach Joe's Seat. Turn right over the stone bridge into the town.

11. Turn left at the T-junction and then left into Lock Up Lane where the troublemakers were held overnight. You may be tempted to browse in the Next Chapter bookshop. Return to the Main Street and turn left and you will see Manchester Square with the Rose and Crown Pub and the Boer War Memorial Fountain. Further along is the old town hall and then St Cuthbert's Church with its stone roof.

12. Return along the main street and turn right, back over the stone bridge and follow the road back to the car park at the Heritage Centre.

HAUXLEY NATURE RESERVE

COAL MINES USED TO COVER THIS AREA AND BROOMSHILL WAS JUST ONE OF THE VILLAGES BUILT TO HOUSE MINERS AND THEIR FAMILIES. WHEN THE COAL HERE WAS DEPLETED AND IT WAS NO LONGER AN ECONOMIC PROPOSITION, THE MINES CLOSED, LEAVING BEHIND A SCARRED LANDSCAPE.

In 1983, the Northumberland Wildlife Trust bought some of the site and turned it into a nature reserve.

Hauxley Nature Reserve was part of Radcliffe opencast coal mine, which was landscaped to produce a lake with islands. There are several bird hides and this is a great place to spot a good variety of birds at different times of the year. Birds seen here include sanderling, dunlin, plover, redshank, lapwing, shoveler and the purple sandpiper. This is also a good place to look out for wild flowers such as kidney vetch, bloody cranesbill, yellow wort and ragged robin. Butterflies and dragonflies can be seen in the meadow areas and there are great crested newts in the small ponds.

Druridge Bay Country Park has also been created from an old opencast mining site and work began on the lake in 1974. This freshwater lake is now surrounded by woods and meadows and has become a haven for swans and ducks. In the meadows and dunes there are many wildflowers including several species of orchid. The Country Park has a café but check on the opening hours.

Nearby is the town of Amble, which can cater for everyday needs as it has banks, local shops and a supermarket. Near the harbour there is a very good ice cream parlour and fish and chips shops. Puffin Cruises run boat trips from the harbour and the lifeboat station is often open to the public. The Tourist Information Centre and public toilets are in the square.

NOTES: If you wish to do the walk the other way round you can park at Druridge Country Park (NE61 5BX). There are no refreshment stops along the way so take some water with you.

THE BASICS

Distance: 5½ miles / 8.9km

Gradient: Small inclines and a few steps

Severity: Easy

Approx time to walk: 4 hrs

Stiles: None

Maps: OS Explorer 332 (Alnwick & Amble) and 325 (Morpeth & Blyth)

Path description: Paths, tracks and beach

Start point: Hauxley Nature Reserve car park (GR NU 285023)

Parking: Hauxley Nature Reserve (NE65 0JR)

Dog friendly: Dogs on leads in nature reserve and country park

Public toilets: At Hauxley Nature Reserve & Druridge Bay Country Park visitor centre

Nearest food: There are lots of cafes, pubs and sandwich shops in Amble and a café at Druridge Bay Country Park which has restricted opening hours

1. Start in Hauxley Nature Reserve car park and go through the gate and turn left. Follow this path round and you will pass the gates that lead to two bird hides. Shortly you will come to a path on your left-hand side that leads out of the reserve and you will then be on the coastal path. Turn right here.

2. Look to the left and you will see Coquet Island with its lighthouse and, in season, 40,000 nesting seabirds including puffins and roseate terns. On the east side of the island is a grey seal colony. Puffin Cruises run boat trips round the island from Amble Harbour.

3. After about a mile and a half, there is an exit from the beach up some steps and this leads you through a wooded area that leads to the car park next to Druridge Bay Visitor Centre, with a café and toilets.

4. From the Visitor Centre take the left-hand path round Ladyburn Lake. Keeping to the low path, walk round the lake and across a footbridge near the top of the lake. Continue along with the lake on your right-hand side. Watch out for swans and ducks. Continue on this path along the edge of Ladyburn Woods, then North Shore Woods and Hadstone Links Wood. Cross a bridge and walk back to the Visitor Centre.

5. From the car park follow the signed footpath to the beach and turn left and enjoy walking back along the bay with its seven miles (11km) of glorious sand.

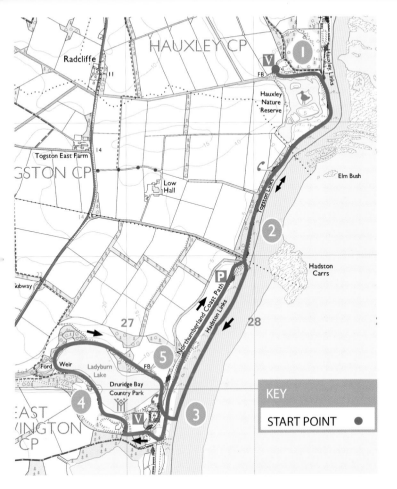

Continue along the beach until you come to an informal parking area, which is an easy way off the beach. Keep on in the same direction, following the coastal path, and eventually you will see the entrance to Hauxley Nature Reserve on your left. Turn right once inside the reserve and follow the path round and you will come to the car park.

HEATHERSLAW & ETAL

THIS IS AN EASY WALK THROUGH DELIGHTFUL SCENERY AND
THE RETURN JOURNEY FROM ETAL TO HEATHERSLAW IS BY
THE HEATHERSLAW NARROW GAUGE STEAM RAILWAY.

The villages of Ford and Etal lie in the Till Valley between the Cheviot Hills and the Scottish Border. Ford village was built for the estate workers at Ford Castle after the original village was demolished as it could be seen from the castle and was considered an eyesore. The old school, now called Lady Waterford Hall, is famous for its murals painted by Lady Louisa Waterford, who included portraits of the villagers who lived in Ford between 1861 and 1883. There is a café in the village shop, a tearoom in the Estate House, antiques in the Horseshoe Forge and a bookshop in the old Estate Drawing Office. Across from the entrance to the village is the Old Dairy which has a coffee shop and sells antiques, and vintage household and garden items.

Along this walk you will visit Heatherslaw Corn Mill, which still produces stone-ground, wholemeal flour from locally grown wheat

(there is an admission charge to see the restored 19th-century mill at work). The tearoom in the old granary overlooks the River Till.

The Church of St Mary the Virgin at Etal is charming and the door is often open, so do look in and slip though the gap at the side of the organ into the South Chapel. Here you will find the tomb of Lord Frederick FitzClarence (1799–1854), the illegitimate son of King William IV, who was originally buried in Ford Church but was moved here in 1876. His wife Lady Augusta and their daughter are both buried beneath the floor of the chapel.

The ruins of Etal Castle, an English Heritage property (admission charge), lie at the far end of Etal village. In 1314, the year of the Battle of Bannockburn, Robert Manners, anxious about protecting his home from the Scots, was granted permission to add curtain walls, corner towers and a gatehouse, turning his house into a fortification.

NOTE: Dogs travel free on the railway and dogs are welcome to sit at the outside tables at the Lavender Tearoom and the Black Bull Pub.

THE BASICS

Distance: 1½ miles / 2.4km

Gradient: Short incline near beginning of walk but mainly flat going

Severity: Easy

Approx. time to walk and return by train: 2 hrs

Stiles: None

Maps: OS Explorer 339 (Kelso, Coldstream & Lower Tweed Valley)

Path description: Mainly tarmacked footpaths, short section of grassy verge

Start point: Heatherslaw Light Railway Car Park off the B6354 at Heatherslaw Mill (GR NT 933383)

Parking: Heatherslaw Light Railway Car Park (TD12 4TJ)

Dog friendly: Keep dogs on leads as livestock in fields and a busy road to cross

Public toilets: At Heatherslaw Corn Mill and in Etal car park

Nearest food: Tearoom at Heatherslaw Corn Mill and the Lavender Tearoom and the Black Bull Pub at Etal

HEATHERSLAW & ETAL WALK

1. Directions start in the car park of the Heatherslaw Light Railway just off the B6354. First of all, go to the Railway Booking Office and find out the times of the trains from Etal back to Heatherslaw and buy a ticket for your return journey. If you do this walk late in the afternoon you may find that there is no suitable train back, so you could take the train to Etal and do the walk backwards. If you do this walk out of season the train may not be running so check first on their website: http://heatherslawlightrailway. co.uk.

2. Walk back to the entrance to the car park and over the bridge to Heatherslaw Corn Mill and enjoy the views of the River Till. At the mill there are toilets, a tearoom and a gift shop.

3. When ready return to the bridge and walk across to the end of the car park where on your left you will see a footpath sign to Etal. Go through the wooden gate and walk along the path.

4. Cross the wooden bridge and continue along the footpath. To your left are views of the river and you may see the steam train chugging along. There is a slight incline here.

5. The path winds through a copse of trees and then bears left.

6. You will come to a wooden gate on your left and see a sign to Erroll Hut Smithy. Go through the gate and cross the road to the footpath on the other side and go left towards Etal.

7. You will soon see the cricket field and pavilion on your right, and when you reach the phone box there is a short distance on the grassy verge until you come to the gates of Etal Manor.

8. Turn right and go through the gates and on your right is the church of St Mary the Virgin, which is usually open. Completed in 1858, it was designed by William Butterfield (1814–1900), who was keen on the Gothic and using different coloured stones, and you can see this in the pink and grey stonework.

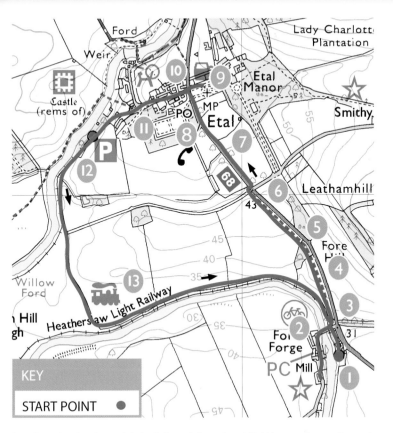

9. From the church turn left, back through the gates of Etal Manor and cross the road. Look ahead and you will see the ruins of Etal Castle.

10. On your left is the Lavender Tearoom with specialities such as lavender scones, singing hinnies and border tart. Dogs are welcome at the outside tables here and across the road at the Black Bull, Northumberland's only thatched pub.

11. Continue through the village to Etal Castle (admission charge) and take the footpath to the castle and the railway. There are public toilets in the car park.

12. When you are ready to take the steam train back to Heatherslaw take the path from the castle to the platform.

13. The journey back takes about 25–30 minutes. Enjoy the views of the river, the countryside and the Cheviot Hills, and look out for swans, ducks and herons.

HEPBURN WOODS

THIS WALK THROUGH HEPBURN WOODS IS A SERIES OF
HILLS, AS THE WIDE WOODLAND PATH TRAVELS UP AND
DOWN THE CONTOURS OF THE LANDSCAPE. SOME RISE
GENTLY AND SLOWLY AND OTHERS ARE STEEP AND LONG
AS YOU FOLLOW THE OLD CARRIAGE DRIVE THROUGH
WHAT WOULD HAVE BEEN A PRIVATE ESTATE BELONGING TO
CHILLINGHAM PARK.

The woodland is tranquil with a variety of broad leaf and coniferous trees and you may be lucky and spy deer in the woods or dashing across the path as I have on quiet days. Across from the entrance to the car park is the ruin of a bastle (a fortified tower house). If you are looking for more strenuous walks, turning right out of the car park and across the cattle grid you will find waymarked routes to the ruins of Ros Castle where, after a very steep climb, you can see seven castles on a clear day and to Hepburn Crag, a lofty sandstone escarpment with the remains of an Iron Age hill fort. On this walk you will see the sites of two Bronze Age graves.

Nearby is Chillingham Castle (admission charge), which has been in the same family line since the 1200s and was a strategic fortress during the Border Wars. The gardens once boasted a pattern of hedges set out by Andre Mollet, gardener at Versailles but local lad, Lancelot 'Capability' Brown (1716–83) swept them all away. The King of France was a guest at Chillingham in the early 1800s and he gave the family a 'fine suite of urns from Versailles'. Jeffry Wyatville (1766–1840), famed for his work at Windsor, designed hedges to display the urns and you can visit this restored Italian Garden. The castle is intriguing with a dungeon, torture chamber and, reputedly, ghosts.

The Wild Cattle of Chillingham have lived there for over 800 years and are survivors of the wild cattle that used to roam Britain's forests. These cattle are not domesticated, are fierce and live by their instincts. The Chillingham bulls will kill any intruder, weak calves or any cow that has been touched by a human. To see the cattle and hear the history of their survival, you can book a guided tour with the Warden. Check their website for details: www.chillinghamwildcattle.com; and for the castle www.chillingham-castle.com.

THE BASICS

Distance: 4½ miles / 7.2km

Gradient: Hilly walk with long steep inclines

Severity: Easy as the paths are good, but the steep inclines may be challenging

Approx time to walk: 3 hrs

Stiles: None

Maps: OS Explorer 332 (Alnwick & Amble) and 340 (Holy Island & Bamburgh)

Path description: Wide woodland paths, stony and uneven in places

Start point: Hepburn Forestry Commission car park (GR NU 073248)

Parking: Hepburn Forestry Commission car park, near Chillingham Castle off A697 south-east of Wooler (NE66 4EG)

Dog friendly: Dogs on leads

Public toilets: Wooler and Alnwick

Nearest food: Chillingham Castle has a tearoom if you pay to visit. There are a couple of local pubs: the Percy Arms in Chatton and the Tankerville Arms in Eglingham

HEPBURN WOODS WALK

1. Take the wide carriage drive on the right-hand side of the information boards and a little way along walk round the side of the gate. Continue along this path, looking to the right for good views of the valley and hills.

2. After about half a mile (1km) you come to a wide path on your right. At the corner, amongst the ferns on your right is a Bronze Age cist and capstone where someone was buried about 2000 BC. This is the junction you will return to towards the end of your walk.

3. Continue along the carriage drive up the hill. The walk is up and down hills all the way to the end. Follow this path for about 1½ miles (2.25km) until you come to a T-junction. Along the way there are variations in the woodland, some open glades and, where there are gaps in the trees, good views to your left. It is on this part of the walk that I have seen deer.

4. At the T-junction look to your left and you will find a second Bronze Age cist and capstone, partially hidden by foliage. Turn right here and continue along the path.

5. This path is also hilly but a bit more open and at times you have views to your left of the hills, valleys and farmland. There are also a variety of birds to be seen and heard. Along here you will come to a fence where you can see the countryside.

6. After around 1½ miles (2.25km) you will arrive back at the junction where you saw the first Bronze Age grave. Turn left here and head back to the gate. Walk around it and head back to the car park.

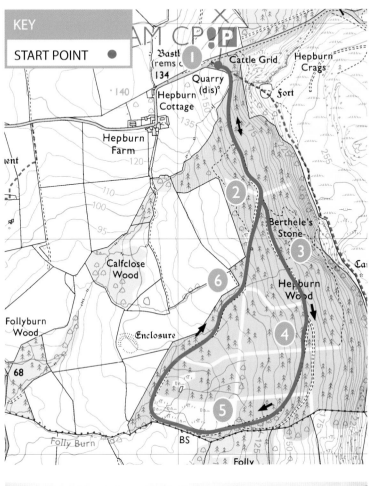

KEY

START POINT ●

HEXHAM

HEXHAM IS AN ATTRACTIVE MARKET TOWN WITH RIVERSIDE WALKS, A MAGNIFICENT ABBEY AND INTERESTING SHOPS. YOU CAN COME HERE BY TRAIN AND DO THIS WALK AS THE STATION IS VERY NEAR THE START POINT AT TYNE GREEN.

The 18th-century nine-arched bridge over the River Tyne was built by Robert Mylne, who also built Blackfriars Bridge in London. In the 19th century, a quarter of a million pairs of gloves were made every year in Hexham and it is said there were four tanneries and sixteen master hatters in the town.

Sport is a popular pastime here with canoeing and fishing on the river, a choice of golf courses and a racecourse. It is also a good base for visiting the Roman sites on Hadrian's Wall such as Housesteads, Vindolanda and the Roman Army Museum.

Hexham has the oldest purpose-built prison in England, now the Old Gaol Museum, and you can explore the dungeon where prisoners would await trial at the Moothall. The Archbishop of York ordered the gaol to be built in 1300 and it was in use until the 1820s when a new gaol was built at Morpeth. However, some prisoners were still held here for offences such as petty theft. In more modern times it has been used as a bank and a solicitors' office.

The building that dominates Hexham is the Abbey which dates from around 1170 to 1250. The cloisters and the north and south transepts date from this period but the east end was rebuilt in the 1860s. It looks over the Market Place where the covered market, the Shambles, was built by Sir Walter Blackett in 1766.

THE BASICS

Distance: 4 miles / 6.4km

Gradient: Flat by river but a few steep hills

Severity: Mostly easy but steep hills in places

Approx time to walk: 3½ hrs

Stiles: None but a railway level crossing

Maps: OS Explore OL 43 (Hadrian's Wall)

Path description: Grassy tracks, paths and pavements

Start point: Tyne Green Country Park (GR NY 938646)

Parking: Tyne Green Country Park, Tyne Green Road, off A6079 just south of the river (NE46 3SG)

Dog friendly: Dogs on leads at level crossing and in town

Public toilets: In Hexham near Tourist Information Centre, St Mary's Wynd and near the play area in the park

Nearest food: Hexham town centre has a good variety of cafés and restaurants

HEXHAM WALK

1. Start in Tyne Green car park and walk across the grass to the riverbank and you will see the bridge on your right. Turn left and follow the path along the riverside. You will soon see a golf course and a children's play area.

2. Near the end of the golf course you will see a sign for the level crossing. Please beware of the dangers here for children and dogs. Follow the instructions and cross the railway line with care. Go through the gate on the other side of the track. Make sure you close the gate.

3. Turn right up a track through the trees signposted public bridleway. On your left you will see a gate to the golf course car park. Continue on and this track will meet up with a made-up road. Turn right up this steep hill. At the T-junction turn left and walk along the pavement. Cross Bowman Drive and then Portland Gardens and go straight on. Pass the West End Methodist Church and the police station.

4. Walk to the junction with the traffic lights. Follow the road to the left past the Army Reserve Centre.

5. Turn left at St Aidan's United Reform Church (St Mary's School on your right). The town centre shops now appear on your left.

6. Turn left at the Beaumont statue and enter the park. Walk along on the main path and you will see a bandstand on your left. Here take the second path towards the Abbey. There is a children's play area on the left.

7. Exit the park through the stone-pillared gates and turn right.

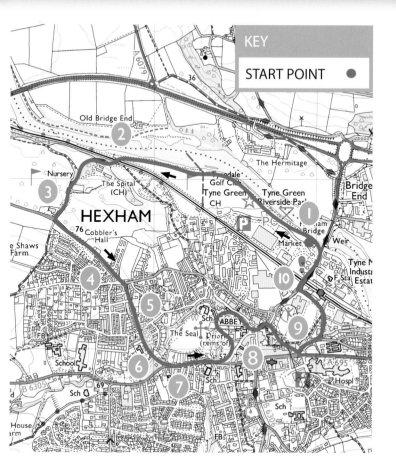

8. Walk along the lane by the Abbey. There is a nice garden on your left. Turn right and walk to the front of the Abbey. On your left is the Market Square. The Abbey is worth a look and it has a nice gift shop. When you have seen the Abbey walk through the Market Place and turn right into Fore Street. There are lots of eateries in this area.

9. Walk to the T-junction and turn left down a hill to the roundabout. Bear left. Bear left again at the next roundabout. Bear left once again at the next roundabout and you will see the railway station on your right.

10. At the roundabout after the station, turn right and cross the Rotary Bridge.

11. At the next roundabout turn left back into the Tyne Green car park where the walk started.

THE HOLY ISLAND OF LINDISFARNE

THERE IS SOME PREPARATION REQUIRED BEFORE YOU DO THIS WALK AS THE HOLY ISLAND OF LINDISFARNE IS REACHED BY TWO MILES (3KM) OF CAUSEWAY WHICH IS ONLY OPEN WHEN THE TIDE IS LOW, AND THIS HAPPENS AT DIFFERENT TIMES EVERY DAY.

You will need to look at the tide tables in the Tourist Information Centre in Seahouses or Berwick-upon-Tweed, the local newspaper or the Northumberland County Council website (www.northumberland.gov.uk) for the safe crossing times. The weather, especially high winds, can influence the tide times so it is best to leave at least one hour before the end of the safe crossing time.

However, do not be put off as this island is magic, stunning and breathtaking. St Aidan travelled from the Island of Iona and set up a monastery in AD 634, a place for contemplation that was isolated by the tides for part of the time, but it was still possible to walk to the mainland or King Oswald's residence in Bamburgh at low tide. St Aidan's statue overlooks the Priory. St Cuthbert was appointed Bishop of Lindisfarne in AD 685 and he used the small St Cuthbert's Isle as a hermitage; a cross marks the spot where the altar stood. Inside St Mary's Church, there is a large wooden carving by Fenwick Lawson depicting the monks carrying St Cuthbert's body to safety when the monks were forced to flee the island during the Viking raids. Eventually, St Cuthbert's body was laid to rest and Durham Cathedral was built on that spot.

During or after this walk around Holy Island, make time to also enjoy the harbour and the picturesque village with its many small shops, cafes and pubs. Interesting places to visit are Lindisfarne Castle and Gertrude Jekyll's garden (both have admission charges), now owned by the National Trust, the Priory, an English Heritage site which also has an admission charge, St Mary's Church, St Cuthbert's Church and Lindisfarne Winery. On the mainland, between the causeway and the A1 is the Barn at Beal, a coffee shop and restaurant with stunning views of the island and Bamburgh Castle.

NOTE: Pilgrims Coffee House welcomes dogs both inside and out and the Manor House Hotel has a dog friendly garden.

THE BASICS

Distance: 3¼ miles / 5.2km

Gradient: Some steep slopes, mostly flat

Severity: Medium

Approx time to walk: 2½ hrs

Stiles: None but two sets of turnstiles

Maps: OS Explorer 340 (Holy Island & Bamburgh)

Path description: Pavements, roads, uneven, grassy, stony and earth paths and tracks

Start Point: Holy Island Village car park (GR NU 127420)

Parking: Holy Island Village car park on the left-hand side as you approach the village (TD15 2SX)

Dog friendly: Dogs on leads

Public toilets: Holy Island Coach Park near St Aidan's Church

Nearest food: There are lots of coffee shops, cafés and pubs to choose from

iStock

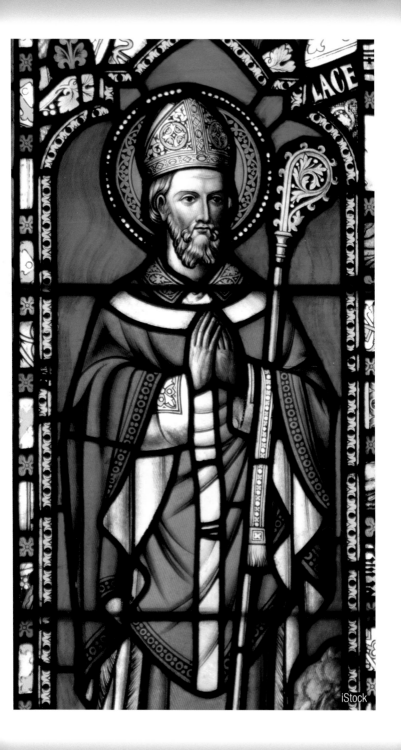

iStock

1. Turn left when you leave the car park and walk along to the T junction. Pilgrims Coffee House will be facing you. Turn right here and walk along past the Lindisfarne Centre with its exhibition of the Lindisfarne Gospels, and the Gospel Garden, and the Post Office, a little further along on your right. Turn left at the T-junction. Along here, on your left-hand side, is St Cuthbert's Church which has a  tiny Boiler House Chapel at the side. Keep straight ahead and St Mary's Church is on your left. Look to your right and you will see St Cuthbert's Island with its cross. This walk cuts through St Mary's churchyard, but do walk further down the slope to the beach as the views are worth it, and then walk back up to the church. Walk through the churchyard keeping to the left of the church. It is worth taking a peek in this church either now or later. You will see on your right St Aidan's statue and the remains of the Priory, which is now managed by English Heritage (admission charge). Turn left along the path and exit through the church gate and you will be in the village with the Celtic Cross in front of you. Turn right and continue down the narrow lane between The Manor House Hotel and the Crown and Anchor Pub. Turn right and go through the metal turnstile and as you walk to the next set of turnstiles look left and you will see the harbour and Lindisfarne Castle. At the next turnstile go straight ahead down to the harbour where you will see upturned boats used as sheds. From here you will see in the distance Bamburgh Castle and perhaps also make out the red and white lighthouse where Grace Darling lived and the white lighthouse on Inner Farne. Continue along until you come to the T-junction and turn right towards the castle. Go through the kissing gate and walk past the castle, keeping it on your right. On your left you will see in the distance Gertrude Jekyll's garden. The castle and garden are owned by the National Trust and there is a charge to visit them. They are certainly worth a visit now or later. Walk along this path and just before you come to a wooden bridge walk up the grassy bank on your left to the higher path and turn left.

2. Walk straight on through the first set of gates and straight on again at the second set of gates. Eventually you will come to a set of gates on your left with a way-post sign. Turn left through the kissing gate. This is mostly a straight path with a couple of bends neat the end. You will come to some farm buildings and a T-junction and turn left here.

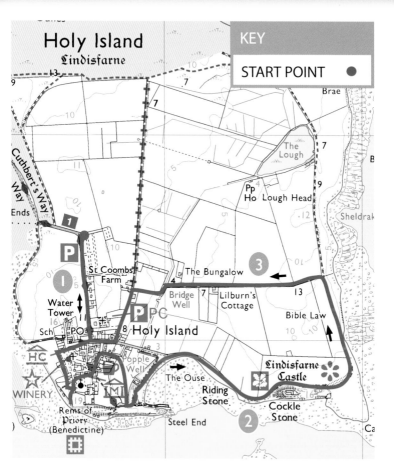

Holy Island
Lindisfarne

KEY

START POINT ●

Brae

The Lough

Pp Ho Lough Head

Sheldrak

Cuthbert's Way

Ends

1

P

I

St Coombs Farm

The Bungalow

3

Water Tower

Sch PO

P PC

Bridge Well

Lilburn's Cottage

13

Bible Law

8 Holy Island

HC

WINERY

Popple Well

The Ouse

Riding Stone

Lindisfarne Castle

Cockle Stone

Rems of Priory (Benedictine)

Steel End

2

Ca

3. Continue along to the T-junction at the end of Sandham Lane and turn right. The Ship Inn is on your right and the National Trust shop is further along on your left. When you come to the Pilgrims Coffee House turn right and walk past the Island Oasis Coffee shop back to the car park.

HOWICK HALL GARDENS

THIS WALK IS IN THE SPLENDID HOWICK HALL GARDENS
AND ARBORETUM, THE HOME OF EARL GREY TEA. AS THIS IS
A PRIVATE ESTATE, THERE IS AN ADMISSION CHARGE.

The grounds are extensive, well maintained and stocked with a large variety of specimen trees from around the world, reflecting the family tradition of tree planters and gardeners.

If you turn right on leaving the ticket office and pass through the entrance gate set in the stone wall, immediately in front of you is Howick Hall. It was originally designed by William Newton (1730–98), a Newcastle architect, and built in 1782. The Hall has been modified several times and the original entrance was on the south side but it was moved to the north side in 1809. The Earl Grey Tea Rooms are in the old ballroom on the left of the Hall and this is the best place to drink this tea, which was blended to suit the water here. The visitor Centre is next to the Tea Rooms and has lots of information about the plants, wildlife and history of the estate.

This walk is an easy and delightful stroll around these famous and extensive gardens, focusing on the East Arboretum. Walking at a leisurely pace with time to stop and look takes almost two hours. All paths on this walk are wide, and of good quality, providing easy walking. However, if you are looking for a more adventurous walk, try the Long Walk from the grounds to the sea and back to the car park. This is 3½ miles (5.5km) and information is available from the ticket office. There is a turnstile as you leave the grounds so you must complete the Long Walk to get back to the car park as you cannot re-enter the grounds any other way. In poor weather conditions, part of this walk can be very muddy and only passable wearing wellies. You can, however, re-enter the gardens and visit the Tea Rooms on production of your ticket when you complete this walk.

THE BASICS

Distance: 1½ miles / 2.4km

Gradient: A few slight inclines

Severity: Easy

Approx time to walk: 2 hrs

Stiles: None

Maps: OS Explorer 332 (Alnwick & Amble)

Path description: Good wide paths

Start point: Howick Hall Gardens car park (GR NU 248176)

Parking: Howick Hall Gardens (NE66 3LB)

Dog friendly: No dogs allowed

Public toilets: Alnwick and for visitors at Howick Hall Gardens

Nearest food: Earl Grey Tea Rooms and a variety of cafés and pubs in Alnwick

HOWICK HALL GARDENS WALK

1. From the car park pass through the entrance gate and turn left. Take second right at post number two. As you walk down this short path, look through the trees on your right and you will see Howick Hall in a very attractive setting. Pass through the gate covered with wire netting to prevent hares and rabbits getting into the Arboretum, remembering to shut it after you. Walk straight down the path and turn left at the crossroads. Keep going, walking over the bridge with iron railings. You come to another rabbit-proof gate. Just after post 44 the path divides. Head down the right-hand path into the valley, keeping Howick Burn on your right. At the bottom of this shallow valley, bear left up the grassy path, eventually passing post 4. In the spring and autumn trees can display some eye-catching colour and fascinating patterns of light and shade. Head for post 5. Here the path divides. Turn right here.

2. Pass post 6 and continue on to post 7. Bear right here and head for post 10. The post shows red and yellow arrows indicating two different walks. Take the path on the left, leading to post 17. Turn right and cross the stone bridge. The path inclines slightly here, passing post 23 on your left. This zone is known as The Banks, and is planted with some interesting trees and shrubs from China and the Himalayas.

3. Continue on this path and at the end of this loop you will re-join the original path. Now retrace your steps back to the car park or perhaps stop for a cup of Earl Grey tea.

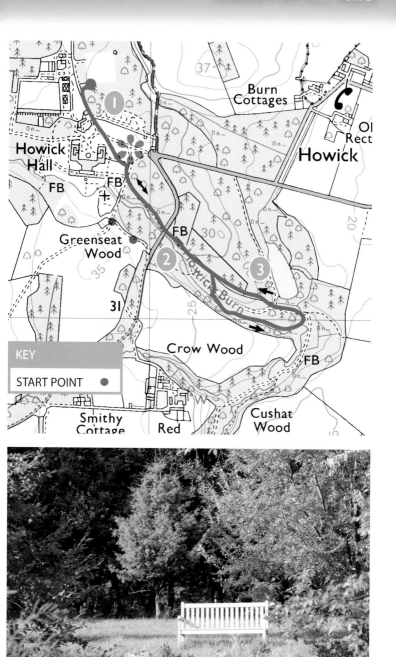

KIELDER WATER & FOREST PARK

HOWEVER FAST YOU WALK YOU WILL NOT SEE KIELDER IN A DAY AS IT IS 250 SQUARE MILES (650 SQ. KM) IN TOTAL, HAS OVER 6,500 SQUARE FEET (600 SQ. M) OF FOREST, 27 MILES (43KM) OF SHORELINE AND A VERY LARGE LAKE. HOWEVER, THERE ARE LOTS OF ROUTES FOR WALKING, CYCLING, MOUNTAIN BIKING AND HORSE RIDING AND THE TRAILS ARE GRADED.

This walk starts off with a boat ride on the *Osprey* ferry and a good walk back, mostly along the shores of the lake. Kielder is a place to return to again and again, and if you wish to stay for a few days you can choose from comfortable lodges, camping or caravanning. There are cafés at Kielder Castle and Tower Knowe and the Boat Inn Restaurant and Bar is at Leaplish Waterside Park.

© Northumbrian Water

This walk starts at Leaplish Visitor Centre, where you can buy a ticket for the Osprey ferry. Start your journey by taking the ferry to Tower Knowe and the walk will follow the lake back to Leaplish. Make sure you check the times of the ferry and the days it is running – see the website at www. visitkielder.com.

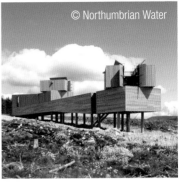

© Northumbrian Water

At Leaplish there is a Birds of Prey Centre with owls, falcons and vultures, a mini-golf course and a children's play area. While on your walk, you may be lucky enough to see red squirrels, otters, roe deer, badgers, bats or ospreys, depending on the time of year. Fungi and meadow flowers, including orchids, all grow here.

Near Kielder Castle Visitor Centre, once the hunting lodge of the Duke of Northumberland, is a Minotaur Maze, and the Kielder Salmon Centre is the largest conservation hatchery in England and Wales: around 900,000 salmon are bred here each year. There are many opportunities for water sports including canoeing, sailing and water skiing. The most exciting new development at Kielder is that they have attained International Dark Sky Park status and their observatory is amazing. Kielder has the darkest skies in England and winter nights are the darkest, so they are best for viewing distant galaxies. In the summer you can view the Milky Way, passing comets and shooting stars and safely see the sun's surface using the solar telescope. You need to book to experience the Observatory and use the telescopes so visit the website (www.kielderobservatory.org) for details.

One visit to Kielder is never enough so if this is your first visit, don't let it be your last.

iStock

THE BASICS

Distance: 5½ miles / 7.75km or 7¾ miles / 12.5km

Gradient: Steep and hilly in parts

Severity: Moderate due to length and inclines

Approx time to walk: 4 hrs or 5 hrs

Stiles: None

Maps: OS Explorer OL42 (Kielder Water & Forest)

Path description: Good paths, trails & tracks

Start point: Leaplish Waterside Park (GR NY 660877)

Parking: Leaplish Waterside Park (NE48 1BT) on Kielder Water

Dog friendly: Dogs on leads

Public toilets: At Leaplish Waterside Park and Tower Knowe Visitor Centre

Nearest food: The Boat Inn, restaurant and bar at Leaplish, a café at Tower Knowe and refreshments available on the *Osprey* ferry

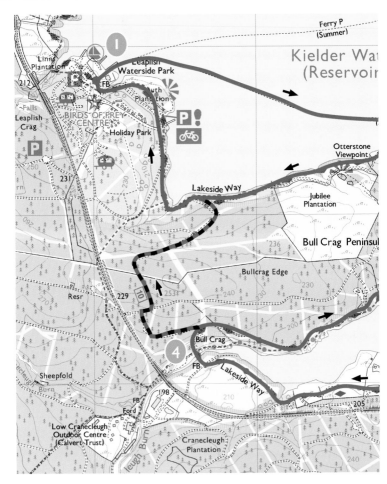

1. Start at Leaplish Visitor Centre. Buy a ticket for the *Osprey* ferry and take the ferry to Tower Knowe. When you get off the ferry there are toilet facilities and refreshments available.

2. This route is well signposted and you have the choice of taking the longer route all the way round Bull Crag peninsula or of taking a shorter route which misses out part of the route around the peninsula.

© Northumbrian Water

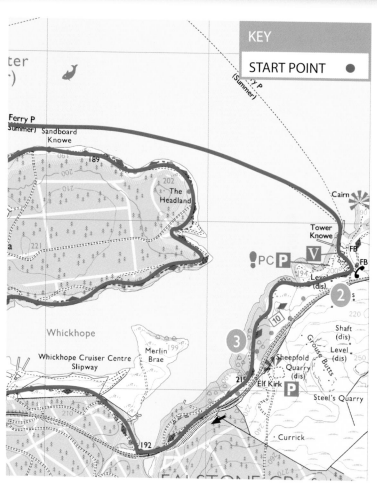

3. Near the Tower Knowe Visitor Centre take the Lakeside Way. You will come to a sign for Elf Kirk and you may wish to climb up here as there are good views of Bull Crag, Merlin Brae and the north shore of the lake. Return to Lakeside Way and continue along and you will see some moored sailing boats at Little Whickhope. You will eventually descend into the Cranecleugh Valley and onto the Bull Crag Peninsula.

© Northumbrian Water

4.	There are a series of bends which take you uphill to the Bull Crag Peninsula. Here you need to choose whether you are going for the long or shorter walk. There is a sign here for a shortcut: take this route for the short walk or take the route that goes all the way round the peninsular for the longer walk. The routes join up at Freya's Cabin and continue past some more art works and a red squirrel hide. Keep along this route and you will arrive back at Leaplish Waterside Park.

© Northumbrian Water

© Northumbrian Water

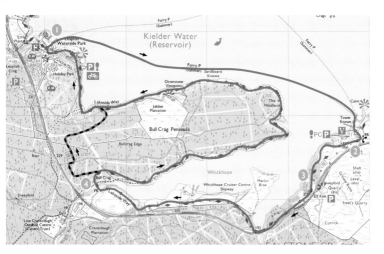

© Northumbrian Water

MORPETH

Morpeth, the 'Gateway to Northumberland', is a bustling market town within easy commuting distance of Newcastle. It is an excellent base for exploring the Northumbrian landscape and coastline and you can catch trains from here to Newcastle upon Tyne, Berwick-upon-Tweed and Edinburgh.

In the town centre there are numerous cafes, restaurants, family tearooms and pubs and a good mix of shops including well-known national names as well as Rutherfords, an independent department store. Just along from Rutherfords is the Town Hall designed by Sir John Vanbrugh (1664–1726) in 1714 who, at the time, was building Seaton Delaval Hall. After a catastrophic fire the Town Hall was rebuilt in 1870. The nearby Bell Tower dates from the 17th century and the bells were first hung in 1706. From here the night curfew rang out at eight o'clock every evening.

Amongst Morpeth's famous people are Admiral Lord Collingwood, Nelson's second-in-command at the Battle of Trafalgar, who moved to Morpeth in 1791, aged 42, after marrying Sarah Blackett. They purchased what is now Collingwood House on Oldgate. Collingwood commanded the *Royal Sovereign*, devastatingly opening the action at midday on 21 October 1805, and took command of the fleet on Nelson's death. Emily Davison, the suffragette who was killed by the king's horse in 1913, is buried in the graveyard of St Mary's Church at Kirkhill, one of the finest 14th-century churches in Northumberland. In the 19th century the churchyard was targeted by grave robbers, who stole valuables from the graves as well as the bodies which were sold for dissection. As a result a watchtower, a hut behind the church, was built by public subscription in 1831 and a guard regularly patrolled the churchyard.

iStock

THE BASICS

Distance: 2 miles / 3.2km

Gradient: Slight inclines

Severity: Easy

Approx time to walk: 1½ hrs

Stiles: None

Maps: OS Explorer 325 (Morpeth & Blyth)

Path description: Paths and pavements

Start point: The Clock Tower in Morpeth (GR NZ 197859)

Parking: There are lots of car parks in Morpeth and they are well signposted (nearest postcode to start point is NE61 1PX)

Dog friendly: Dogs on leads

Public toilets: In Morpeth

Nearest food: Morpeth has a good variety of tearooms, coffee shops, pubs and restaurants

MORPETH WALK

1. Start at the bell tower at the junction of Newgate Street, Newmarket and Bridge Street in the town centre. With your back to the side with the steps head down Oldgate towards Oldgate Bridge. If you look to the right, just before the bridge, there is a large house built with sandstone. This was the home of Admiral Lord Collingwood, Nelson's second-in-command at the Battle of Trafalgar. Now walk over the bridge and turn sharp right. A short distance along go through the gate set in the flood defence wall and walk along the path known as Lady's Walk, with the river on your right. This is a good stretch of path along the river bank with views across the river. Keep on, passing the stepping stones while admiring the well-kept terrace gardens on the opposite bank. When you arrive at the footbridge there is a blue painted lamp post

on the left, an example of a sewer gas destructor lamp, invented by Joseph Webb in the 1890s.The lantern contained three gas mantles burning mains gas which created a strong up draught, drawing methane sewer gas up the lamp post from the sewer below ground which was then burned off.

2. Walk over the footbridge which was named the Wansbeck Bridge when built in 1881. After years of successive flood damage the present bridge was reopened in 1984 and is known as the 'Skinnery' Bridge as it was once adjacent to the tannery. At the opposite end, walk up the short tarmac lane, turn right at the top and continue up the gentle incline to the road end. Turn right and head down towards the town centre. On the left, about halfway down the road you pass a well-worn screen built in the Romanesque style with a splendid avenue of lime trees leading up to the church of Saint James the Great. Continue walking down, passing through the traffic lights, and at the end turn left into the Market Place. On the opposite side is the Town Hall, designed by Sir John Vanbrugh in 1714.

3. Walk down Bridge Street, with Rutherford's Department Store on your right and Sanderson Arcade on the left. Almost at the end of Bridge Street there is a red post box in front of the Chantry and the Tourist Information Centre. Turn right, passing

between the Chantry and the mock Tudor style corner building, onto the footbridge crossing the Wansbeck. Over on the left is the Telford Bridge (New Bridge), built in 1831. Continue down Wansbeck Street and bear left, walking past The Waterford Lodge, until you come to Carlisle Park on your right, with its imposing entrance. Just inside the entrance is an information panel, and the well-maintained William Turner Garden is just behind the greenhouses. Turner was born in Morpeth around 1508 and is considered the founding father of English botany. When you are ready, head for the riverside path. The path from the entrance swings to the right up a steep incline and then drops down to the river. Take the path nearest the river and you will come to a green painted footbridge, The Elliot Bridge was erected by public subscription in 1925, and rebuilt in 1982. Turn left and continue along the path and at the sign for Matheson Gardens bear left onto the riverside path. You arrive back at Oldgate Bridge which you crossed previously. Up the steps and turn right and you are back at the clock tower.

OTTERBURN

OTTERBURN WAS THE SITE OF A FAMOUS BATTLE IN 1388 BETWEEN THE PERCYS AND THE EARL OF DOUGLAS. THE SCOTS WON THE BATTLE BUT JAMES, EARL OF DOUGLAS WAS KILLED AND SIR HENRY PERCY, BETTER KNOWN AS HARRY HOTSPUR, WAS CAPTURED.

It is thought that those killed in this battle are buried at St Cuthbert's Church in Elsdon as in 1810 over a hundred skeletons were found buried against the north wall of the church, and in 1877 more remains were found. The site of the Battle of Otterburn is commemorated by the Percy Cross and it is said that the stones in the porch of St John's Church in Otterburn are part of this old monument. The present Percy Stone marking the battle site was erected in 1777. St John's Church was designed by John Dobson (1785–1865), a famous Newcastle architect.

There appears to have been a mill at Otterburn for hundreds of years. In 1821, William Waddell modernised the mill and produced yarns and tweeds from local wool, and the mill remained in the family for four generations.

The mill is set in beautiful countryside near the border with Scotland. It is now a retail outlet offering a wide range of products including rugs, woollens and outdoor clothing. The Weavers Coffee Shop and Restaurant serve home-cooked meals using local produce. There is some interesting machinery from the old mill in a small museum area where you can find out how cloth was once produced here.

THE BASICS

Distance: 3½ miles / 5.6km

Gradient: Slight inclines

Severity: Easy

Approx time to walk: 2½ hrs

Stiles: None

Maps: OS Explorer OL 42 (Kielder Water & Forest)

Path description: Woodland path and pavement and roads

Start point: Otterburn Mill (GR NY 887927)

Parking: Otterburn Mill car park, on B6320 just south of Otterburn (NE19 1JT)

Dog friendly: Dogs on leads

Public toilets: Otterburn (on the main road)

Nearest food: Otterburn Mill Weavers coffee shop; restaurant and café on the main road

OTTERBURN WALK

1. Start in Otterburn Mill car park and here you can have a look in the mill shop and enjoy some refreshment in the Weavers Coffee Shop or a picnic. Take some time to have a look at the old mill machinery inside and outside. At the end of the mill buildings, look around the corner at the rare examples of 18th-century tenter frames. Washed cloth was hooked onto the tenter hooks to dry and stretch. From this came the expression 'to be on tenterhooks'.

2. Walk over to the entrance to the picnic area and walk through this picnic spot to the far end. On your right are a gate and a wooden bridge. Go through the gate and over the bridge and turn right.

3. Follow the well-worn path through the small wood with the Otter Burn on your left and a fence on your right. You will come to a main road. Cross the road with care and turn left towards the stone bridge. There are public toilets nearby.

4. Cross the bridge and continue along the main road until you come to the Church of St John the Evangelist on your right.

5. Enter the church and inside the porch are the remains of the old Percy Cross that marked the site of the Battle of Otterburn. A new monument was erected on the battlefield in 1777. This church has attractive stained-glass windows depicting three Northumbrian Saints: St Cuthbert, St Ethelburga and St Aidan.

6. Turn right when leaving the church and you will see the Otterburn Millennium Green picnic area. Continue along the road. Cross over the road by the bus depot, keeping to the main road.

7. Continue along the footpath here for about a mile, passing fields, a few houses and more fields until you come to a sign to Otterburn Battlefield. The entrance is on your right (there is parking here if you prefer to drive to the Battlefield). Here you can see the site of the battle and if you wish to walk a little further,

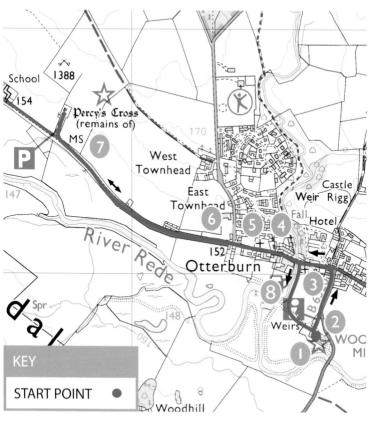

KEY

START POINT ●

the remains of the 1777 Percy Cross. There are English Heritage information boards about the battle.

8. Return to the main road and turn left and make your way back to St John's Church.

9. Walk past the church and over the stone bridge. Continue along the main road until you come to the Border Reiver Village Store, which has a café. Turn right, carefully crossing the main road, and follow this road back to Otterburn Mill and the car park.

ROTHBURY

ROTHBURY, KNOWN AS 'THE CAPITAL OF COQUETDALE', IS AN INTERESTING NORTHUMBERLAND MARKET TOWN WITH A WIDE RANGE OF LOCAL SHOPS WHERE YOU WILL BE SERVED WITH OLD-FASHIONED CHARM AND COURTESY. ALTHOUGH BUILT WITH MELLOW SANDSTONE, SOME BUILDINGS HAVE A STERN, SEVERE APPEARANCE LIKE THOSE OF MANY BORDER TOWNS.

The name of Rothbury is said to come from the Celtic word rath, signifying 'a cleared spot', and this seems plausible as Rothbury was once surrounded by forest. King John (1167–1216) visited Rothbury in 1201 and granted it a charter for a market, and in 1205 he gifted it to Robert FitzRoger, Baron of Warkworth. Consequently, the town gained importance as a centre for dealing in cattle and wool, as it was situated at a crossroads and a ford over the River Coquet.

In former times, the people here were considered to be amongst the wildest and most uncivilised in the county, with a reputation for fighting, gaming and drinking. Rothbury even had its own hooligan! Thomas Hulligan was a wheelwright, and to increase his business he placed jagged stones near the Coquet Bridge. The locals were well aware of this but visitors were often caught out and needed repairs to their damaged wheels. Thomas would come quickly to their rescue. Hulligan died under the wheels of a carriage in Newcastle when he staggered, roaring drunk, from a tavern.

The Coquet Bridge has four arches, three of which are reinforced by heavy chamfered piers. The fourth arch was added in the 18th century to accommodate the river as it widened, and the road, as it gained importance as a corn road from Hexham to the port of Alnmouth.

Nearby is Cragside, the home of Lord William George Armstrong (1810–1900), the Tyneside industrialist, who founded the Armstrong Whitworth engineering empire.

Perhaps better known for manufacturing armaments, the company also made hydraulic cranes, bridges and steam-driven pumps and supplied hydraulic pumping engines to operate London's Tower Bridge. The lakes on his estate were used to generate hydro-electricity to power incandescent bulbs supplied by Joseph Swan (1828–1914). The house, designed by Richard Norman Shaw, RA (1831–1912) stands on a rocky platform perched above the Debdon Burn. Cragside and its magnificent gardens are administered by the National Trust and open to visitors (there is an admission charge for non-members).

THE BASICS

Distance: 2¼ miles / 3.6km

Gradient: Mostly flat, small inclines

Severity: Easy but stepping stones to cross the river may be challenging for some

Approx time to walk: 2 hrs

Stiles: None but there are stepping stones to cross the river

Maps: OS Explorer 332 (Alnwick & Amble)

Path description: Pavements, earth paths and tracks

Start point: Cow Haugh car park (GR NU 057015)

Parking: Cow Haugh by the riverside (near NE65 7RX) and Beggars Rigg on the B6341 (near NE65 7TS)

Dog friendly: Dogs on leads; they need to be happy crossing the stepping stones

Public toilets: Bridge Street, Rothbury

Nearest food: Lots of places to eat in this market town including tearooms and pubs

1. Park at Cow Haugh car park. Exit the car park onto the foot path parallel to the road and turn left (with the river on your left) and head for Rothbury Bridge. It was rebuilt around the 16th century and widened in 1759, 1864 and 1927. The date 1759 and the initials W.O. (William Oliphant, a Rothbury mason) are said to be visible low on the east face.

2. Cross the road and keep on straight ahead. A road sign reads A6079 Hexham. The footpath is on a gentle upward slope and when you reach the Coquetdale Hotel turn left down a rather nondescript rough lane which takes you past the livestock market. This leads onto a short narrow path taking you to the river and the stepping stones.

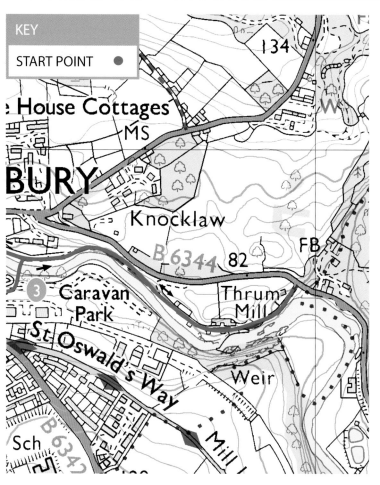

3. When you reach the opposite side turn right and head for Thrum Mill, approximately half a mile (1km). The first few yards are on a hard surface which soon gives way to a woodland path parallel to the river known as 'Lovers Walk', a public bridleway. The bridleway passes between the mill buildings to the mill where the Coquet flows through a narrow channel in a wooded valley. Although the mill and the adjacent buildings are beside a public bridleway, they are private property. The mill, abandoned for fifty years, was featured in the TV series *Restoration Man* in January 2013 . After looking at the mill retrace your steps to the stepping stones.

4. At the stepping stones walk straight ahead and bear to the left, proceed along the path marked 'riverside' which runs adjacent to the river. (The sign reading 'private road' refers to the road immediately in front of the houses on your right.) When

you reach Rothbury Bridge, after just a few yards, turn to the right and walk up the path at the side of the bridge, joining the main road at the top.

5. Cross over and head for the town centre. On the way, just on the left, are public toilets. Ahead is Barclays Bank, an interesting reminder of Rothbury's past. Look up above the second floor and you'll see the name North Eastern Bank carved into the stonework. Originally it was the Alnwick and County Bank and then, in 1875, the North Eastern Banking Company. Rebuilt in 1893, the facade in renaissance style offers reassurance to its customers with echoes of strength and reliability transmitted through its rusticated stonework. The clear message to the local people was, 'your money is safe here'.

6. Now turn left and stay on the left-hand side. A few yards further along is the Market Place. In the corner is the Rothbury United Reform Church, originally built as a Congregational Church in 1896. Face the church and walk down the lane on the right, passing a row of cottages known as Model Buildings, built by Lord Armstrong of Cragside in the 1870s. At the end of the lane, cross over the footbridge and return to the car park.

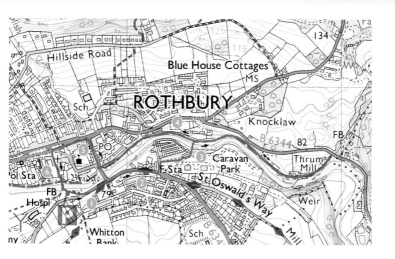

THE UNION CHAIN BRIDGE

THIS WALK STARTS AT THE CHAIN BRIDGE HONEY FARM, HORNCLIFFE, WHERE THERE IS AN INTERESTING EXHIBITION ABOUT THE UNION CHAIN BRIDGE, WHICH WAS OPENED ON 26 JULY 1820.

The designer, Captain Samuel Brown RN, rode across the bridge in a curricle (a small, two-wheeled chariot) followed by twelve carts, fully loaded, to demonstrate its strength. Today it is the oldest surviving suspension bridge in Europe.

The bridge can be crossed on foot or by one vehicle at a time, and traverses the River Tweed, the border between England and Scotland. If you wish, you can join the Friends of the Union Chain Bridge and help support its conservation. This walk takes you over the border into Scotland and to Paxton House, a Georgian mansion, designed by John Adam (1721-1792) and famed for its Chippendale furniture. There is a charge for admission to the grounds and you can pay extra for a guided tour of the house or a boat trip along the river depending on the time of year. Tickets are available from their gift shop. Check their website for more information: www.paxtonhouse. co.uk. The tearoom at Paxton House is in the old stables and serves hearty cooked breakfasts and home-made hot lunches as well as scones and cakes.

Entrance to the Honey Farm is free, as is their car park. As well as a gift shop, there is a display of old farm machinery and a Vintage Museum. Their café is on an old double-decker bus and serves a good selection of sandwiches, delicious home-made cakes and honey ice cream.

THE BASICS

Distance: 2½ miles / 4km

Gradient: Some long and steep hilly stretches

Severity: This is mostly an easy walk but the two stiles might be challenging

Approx time to walk: 2 hrs (not including stops at attractions)

Stiles: Two

Maps: OS Explorer 346 (Berwick-upon-Tweed)

Path description: Roads, forest tracks, field paths, wooden bridges, loose flint paths

Start point: Chain Bridge Honey Farm (GR NT 935507)

Parking: Chain Bridge Honey Farm car park just north of Horncliffe, off the A698 (TD15 2XT) or on road by entrance

Dog friendly: Dogs on leads

Public toilets: Toilets at the Honey Farm and Paxton House for visitors

Nearest food: Old Bus Café at the Honey Farm and the Stables Tearoom at Paxton House. There is a pub in Horncliffe village and one in Paxton village

THE UNION CHAIN BRIDGE WALK

1. Leave the Honey Farm and turn right towards the Union Chain Bridge; just before you walk across you will see the England sign on your right. On the far side you will see the Scotland sign.

2. Walk straight ahead along the road. You will pass a couple of entrances to houses and see a sign reading 'Tweedhill'. Near a bend you will see the entrance to Tweedhill Lodge with stone pillars and a private road sign. To the left of this entrance is a public footpath with a signpost to Paxton. Go through the gate and follow this path to the end, where it turns left down some steep steps to a wooden bridge.

3. Cross the bridge and go up some steep steps and, bearing left, go through the gate. Walk along this rough track and at the end you will see a road. Turn right and walk along the road, being careful to look out for traffic.

4. You will pass a field gate and track but keep to the road and a few yards further on there is a stone-pillared gateway on the right. On the other side of the road there is a sign to Nabdean.

5. Walk down the driveway, bearing left at the fork. When you eventually come to the T-junction, turn right and follow the path which turns into a grassy path just further along. The cottage on the left is private property, so please respect their privacy.

6. A little further on, there is a bridge on the right. Cross over the bridge and walk up the track with a wood on your left and a wire field fence on your right. At the end of the fence, walk across the wide grassy parkland to the car park. To continue this walk you need to go to the gift shop and buy a grounds ticket and a ticket for a tour of Paxton House if you wish to see inside the House. The tearoom is in the courtyard and worth a visit, as is the garden at the back of the house, which is not on the route of this walk.

7. When you have completed your visit here return to the car park and walk up the main drive. Cross over the stone bridge, turning right along a well-worn path which declines steeply towards the end. The Linn Burn is on your right, running along the bottom of the quarry and eventually flowing into the River Tweed.

8. Cross the wooden bridge and you will see the River Tweed on your left-hand side. Walk along the river bank. The path varies here from grassy to uneven walking over large stones. Along the way you will see the Salmon Lookout Tower where the fishermen would stand watching out for shoals of salmon in the river. You will then see the fishing shiel (i.e. shelter) and nearby, a small museum on your right. Eventually, you will see the Union Chain Bridge in the distance.

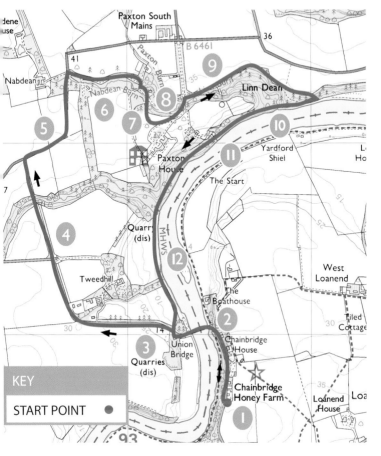

KEY

START POINT ●

9. Continue along the path until you arrive at a fork where the main path goes right. Turn right up the path and the left towards the bird hide. Pass the hide, cross over the wooden bridge and follow the path around to the right, between the wall and the woodland. You will soon come to a stile set in a doorway in the wall.

10. Cross this stile and bear left to the next stile and cross over it.

11. Walk along the path with the river on your left. One or two sections of this riverside path can be narrow and uneven, with occasional muddy patches, depending on the weather. There is a seat about halfway along with good views of the river.

12. Walk along to the Union Chain Bridge and go through the gate. Cross over the bridge, turn right and follow the road back to the Honey Farm.

WALLTOWN QUARRY

Because of the linear nature and rough terrain of the area, Hadrian's Wall is not an easy walk. So with this in mind, for those who would like to see and touch the wall, look across hundreds of miles of open country and imagine what it would have been like standing there almost 2,000 years ago, Walltown Quarry has advantages as a base for an undemanding but interesting day out.

The walk described here, in the Nature Reserve, is a stroll around a slowly maturing wildlife habitat. There is outdoor seating for family picnics and the famous Roman Army Museum nearby.

All paths in Walltown are good, made up with gravel or compacted earth, mainly level with a few dips and gentle inclines. The exception is the path up to the section of wall on the crags, which entails a steep climb, walking on grass. Depending on your rate of ascent this could take 10 or 15 minutes from the gate to the wall but it is worth the effort. If you do this on a bright sunny day you might be fascinated by the view, but on a cold damp rainy day you are more likely to be aware of the bleakness and to wonder how on earth the garrison soldiers kept their sanity through the dark Northumbrian winters. If you visit Vindolanda museum, you will find out about requests sent back home for extra socks. A visit to the Roman Army Museum and Roman Vindolanda will show you what life was like on the northern frontier of the Roman Empire.

THE BASICS

Distance: 1½ miles / 2.4km

Gradient: A few dips and inclines but a steep climb up the crags to Hadrian's Wall

Severity: Easy but the climb to the Wall is challenging

Approx time to walk: 1½ hrs

Stiles: None

Maps: OS Explorer OL 43 (Hadrian's Wall)

Path description: Good footpaths but grassy climb to the Wall

Start point: Walltown Quarry car park (GR NY 669659)

Parking: Walltown Quarry car park (pay and display; postcode CA8 7JD), to the north of the B6318 north-west of Haltwhistle

Dog friendly: Dogs on leads

Public toilets: Walltown Quarry car park

Nearest food: Walltown Quarry car park

WALLTOWN QUARRY WALK

1. Start in Walltown Quarry pay and display car park, which has picnic tables and toilets. There is a family-run takeaway refreshment facility with a wide choice of food and ice cream. You can also pick up a free Walltown map and other leaflets here. Before you start your walk it is best to visit the Roman Army Museum (admission charge) and see what life was like for a Roman soldier stationed on Hadrian's Wall.

2. Head for the gate, signed Labyrinth, in the left-hand corner of the car park (with Walltown Centre on your right).

3. You will come to a junction in the path. Bear left and just around the corner the path divides again; take the narrow right hand grassy path.

4. At the end of this path turn right. This path meanders a bit through a pleasant landscape; turn second right along a grassy path which will bring you to the main National Trail route.

5. At the junction bear left and follow the path up to the gate at the end. Go through the gate and turn left; this is a fairly steep ascent up to the restored section of the Wall.

6. On reaching the Wall enjoy the views. Return down the grassy path, go through the gate and head back down the track.

7. At the fork continue straight on and bear left at the next junction. Quarry Lake should be on your left. When you get to the end of the path go through the gate and back into the car park.

WOOLER

The township of Wooler, nestling at the foot of the Cheviot Hills, is situated on a slope leading down to Wooler Water, looking out over a wide vista with the fertile valley of the Till in the foreground and the Kyloe Hills in the distance.

In the past, Wooler was known for corn production, most of which was exported along with wool from sheep grazing on the slopes of the Cheviot Hills. In previous centuries wool was big business. In many ways Wooler hasn't changed much over time. In *A History of Northumberland* (1922) it is described as consisting 'of one long straggling street, with some minor offshoots', with the recent 'building of some villas on the ground which falls away from the main street towards the river'.

Walking up Main Street, apart from the goods in the shops and modern styles of display, little appears to have changed. On entering some of the shops you can feel transported back to the 1950s and 60s, when time didn't seem to matter, the customer was important and there was time to chat. Wooler is an excellent centre for walking, cycling and horse riding. Popular with walkers, the St Cuthbert's Way footpath running from Melrose to Holy Island passes through Wooler.

Glendale is said to be the inspiration for the popular Postman Pat children's television series written by John Cunliffe, who ran the Wooler mobile library service in the early 1950s.

On this walk you will see some rock carvings that are thousands of years old, made perhaps by Neolithic or Early Bronze Age people. They are called 'cup and ring' marks. The 'cup' is the depression in the middle and this is surrounded by circles etched into the stone called 'rings'. No one is quite sure of their significance.

THE BASICS

Distance: 4 miles / 6.4km

Gradient: Very steep to begin with and then gentler slopes

Severity: Easy but more challenging due to the steep part at the beginning

Approx time to walk: 2½ hrs

Stiles: One

Maps: OS Explorer 340 (Holy Island & Bamburgh)

Path description: Country tracks and uneven paths

Start point: Lay-by on Brewery Road near the cricket ground (GR NT 999278)

Parking: Lay-by near the cricket ground on Brewery Road, just off the A697 to the east (nearest postcode NE71 6RP); see walk directions for more details

Dog friendly: Dogs on leads where there is livestock

Public toilets: In Wooler

Nearest food: Tearooms and pubs in Wooler

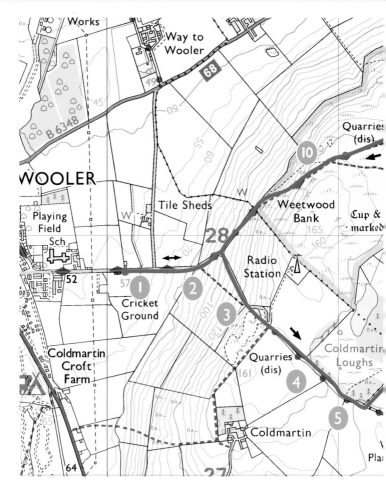

1. To reach the starting point turn off the A697 Morpeth–Coldstream road into Brewery Road. On the corner is the Riverside Bar. Drive straight up, passing Glendale Middle School on the left and park in the lay-by further up on the right, by the cricket ground. This walk comprises some fairly long straight country tracks with a steep incline to start with giving way to fairly flat walking with occasional uneven areas. Please keep to the paths.

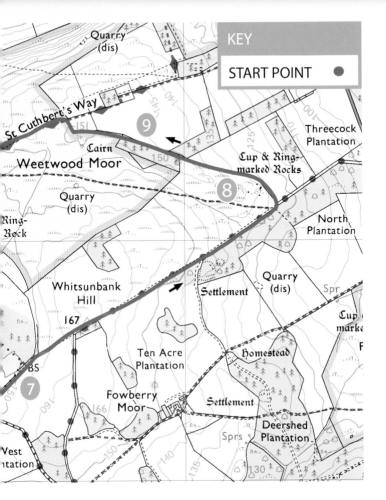

KEY

START POINT ●

2. Start walking up the tarmac road (heading east, away from the centre of Wooler). This is a steep incline. When you pass the radio transmitter on the left, the tarmac gives way to a track. Keep on walking along this track until you arrive at a crossroads.

3. There is a farm gate on your right. Turn left and continue up the track, for around twenty yards, then turn sharp left up the farm track, ignoring the yellow waymarker.

4. Continue up the farm track until you reach another farm gate, and pass through the gate, shutting it after you. The track bears to the right and the wood should be on your right as you turn the corner. The next section is a long straight path, slightly downhill.

5. Walk right as you turn the corner, then down the farm track with gorse bushes on both sides, through a galvanised farm gate.

6. The track eventually gives way to a tarmac roadway and at this point the entrance gate to Fowberry Moor Farm is on your right.

7. Further down on the left before the cattle grid there is a path and signpost saying Weetwood Moor and Wooler. Take this path. On this section there are some wayposts with white-painted tops. At the fifth post look over to your right and hidden in the ferns there is a post marked 'no open access'. Just behind this post there is an outcrop of rock with visible cup and ring markings.

8. After viewing the cup and ring markings return to the path and continue walking across the moor to a wooden gate. Go through and turn sharp right. This path tends to be indistinct, but you will see a stile post ahead, so aim for this. Cross over the stile; continue straight ahead keeping the Cheviot Hills in front of you and walk on through the heather, coming to some marshy ground on your right.

9. At this point there is a yellow waymarker post. Continue straight on until you arrive at a T-junction. Go left here for a few yards and then take a path bearing right. Keep on with the radio transmitter on your left.

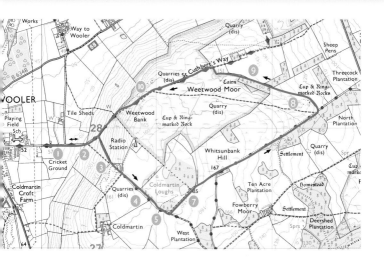

0. Another path merges in from the left; continue on and shortly you come to the top of the bank. Take the path through the ferns straight in front and continue down the bank, arriving at the tarmac road, then continue down until you arrive back at your starting point.

ACKNOWLEDGEMENTS

I would like to thank the following for contributing walks for this book: John Sanderson and Hugh Graham for Craster and Dunstanburgh; Roger and Sandra Smith for Wooler; and John Sanderson for Amble and Warkworth, Howick Hall Gardens, Morpeth, Rothbury and Walltown. Thank you also to David and Hilary Lauckner for their ideas and advice.

I am grateful to Northumbrian Water for permission to reproduce images of Kielder Water and Forest Park in this book; and a special thank you to Janine Scott, Corporate Affairs Advisor for her help and also to Northumberland National Park and the Forestry Commission. Many businesses and individuals gave permission for photographs, ideas for walks and information on local history and I thank you all for your contributions to this book, especially the Carriages Tea Room, Dunstanburgh Golf Club, Hauxley Nature Reserve, Heatherslaw Light Railway, the Honey Farm, Howick Hall and Gardens, the Loovre café, the Next Chapter, Otterburn Mill and Paxton House.

Photographs: Kielder Water and Forest Park ©Northumbrian Water; all other photographs © K. Sanderson unless otherwise stated.

BIBLIOGRAPHY

Emett, C. (1994). 100 Walks in Northumberland, Ramsbury: Crowood Press.

Kristen, C. (1993). Ghost Trails of Northumbria, Leeds: Casdec Ltd.

Reid, M. and Ives, J.A. (2002). Town Trails, Northumbria, Harrogate: Innway Publications.

iStock